The Art of Business Process Modeling

The Business Analyst's Guide to Process
Modeling with UML & BPMN

by

Martin Schedlbauer

The Art of Business Process Modeling

Published by
The Cathris Group
Sudbury, Massachusetts
www.cathris.com

Printed in the United States of America

Library of Congress Cataloging-in-Publication Data

Schedlbauer, Martin J.
  The Art of Business Process Modeling
M. Schedlbauer
  p.cm
Includes index.

ISBN 1-450-54166-6
EAN-13 978-1-45054-166-4

1. Project Management. 2. Computer Software – Development 3. Information Technology – Management
4. Business Requirements Analysis

Table of Contents

PREFACE

Building information systems without understanding the business context is a risky endeavor and one that often turns into a costly mistake. Information systems and their requirements must be analyzed within the context of the business. We need to understand business processes if we expect to successfully automate them – either in part or in whole.

This book is principally about business process modeling, although I have also included information on business process management and business process analysis. The approach outlined in based on the *PROMAP* methodology that I developed and have successfully used in my consulting engagements for many years. It is targeted to anyone who needs to model any kind of process or workflow, including Business Analysts, Business Architects, Systems Analysts, and Software Developers.

The selection of the content of this book is principally drawn from my consulting engagements where I learned which techniques are actually important. I am particularly grateful to the thousands of people that have attended my workshops over the past twenty years and my Information Systems students at Northeastern University; I am certain that I have learned as much from them as they have from me.

The diagrams in this book were prepared using Sparx' Systems excellent *Enterprise Architect* tool. The book itself was typeset using *Microsoft Word*. Finally, the mind maps were done using *FreeMind*, a great open source utility.

Martin Schedlbauer, Ph.D.

Boston, Massachusetts

January 2010

ABOUT THE AUTHOR

Dr. Martin Schedlbauer is an accomplished software architect, business analyst, lecturer and corporate consultant. He has been designing software systems since 1991. In addition, he frequently presents seminars on software engineering, business analysis, and requirements management to corporate clients throughout the world. Previously, Dr. Schedlbauer served as CTO for Global Services at BEA Systems, Inc. where he led the development of the organization's system development methodology and as founder and CEO/CTO for Technology Resource Group, Inc., a global IS education firm.

Dr. Schedlbauer lectures on business informatics at Suffolk University, Northeastern University, Boston University, and the University of Massachusetts Lowell. He actively conducts research in applied software engineering and nomadic human computer interaction. Dr. Schedlbauer holds B.S., M.Sc. and Ph.D. degrees in Computer Science from the University of Massachusetts Lowell.

To have Martin present a customized training program for your organization, contact him through *The Cathris Group* at **martins@cathris.com** or visit **www.cathris.com**.

ABOUT THE CATHRIS GROUP

The Cathris Group is a technology education and consulting practice helping IT organizations maximize their effectiveness through the practical application of modern and proven systems development approaches. Founded in 2001 by Dr. Martin Schedlbauer, The Cathris Group has built a strong reputation for excellence in training, business analysis and software implementation. Its cost-effective programs have been delivered world-wide for a diverse set of clients.

Our training programs are drawn from our consulting engagements and are therefore presented in a practical manner with real-world examples. Our course materials are written in-house and can be tailored to each client. We are skilled in all aspects of modern software development, including object-oriented modeling, agile methods, UML, the Business Analysis Body of Knowledge (BABOK), business process modeling (BPM), use case analysis, and implementation with Java, EJB, C#, .NET, XML, and relational databases.

We offer a variety of services to our clients, including:

- Business Process Modeling
- Agile Project Coaching
- Courseware Authoring
- Executive Briefings

The Cathris Group serves small to medium software organizations across the U.S., Canada, and Europe, spanning across many industries including financial services, higher education, pharmaceutical, and manufacturing.

Training Programs

Business Systems Analysis

- Essential Business Systems Analysis
- Requirements Elicitation and Documentation
- Requirements Management
- Use Cases & User Stories
- Data and Information Modeling
- Workflow & Process Modeling with UML and/or BPMN
- Information Systems Analysis & Design
- Modeling with Enterprise Architect & UML
- Prototyping for Requirements Discovery

Software Development

- Object-Oriented Analysis & Design with UML
- Iterative & Agile Development
- Scrum
- Relational Database Design & SQL
- Essential UML for IT Professionals
- Introductory and Advanced Java
- Introductory and Advanced C++
- Working with XML

1 ESSENTIAL CONCEPTS

Chapter Objectives

- Understand the steps of business process management
- See how the *BABOK* views business process modeling
- Explore the differences between modeling, analysis, and drawing
- Identify the main components of the business architecture
- List business process modeling and visualization tools

Information systems have become a critical part of the infrastructure of most, if not all, businesses, government organizations, and even individual households. To be useful, an information system must integrate and align with the way the business conducts its operations. By necessity this means that information systems construction requires an understanding of the organization's procedures, operations, and processes. Articulating, modeling, and managing business processes and workflows are pre-conditions to successful automation.

Business processes are part of the fabric of the business and represent a strategic and critical intellectual asset that needs to be understood and proactively managed. Processes are often cross-functional and involve multiple systems, software applications, and human assets – including employees, customers, partners, and vendors. Processes must be formally defined and documented so that they can be practiced uniformly and consistently across the organization. Explicit articulation of processes is essential so that the processes truly become intellectual property of the organization rather than being tied to a specific individual.

Business process modeling (or *BPM* for short) is the activity of eliciting, documenting, visualizing, and analyzing work procedures within an organization. To be successful, the business analyst must possess the necessary modeling skills and business knowledge to perform these tasks.

The first step in business process modeling is capturing and articulating the processes. This is done through process modeling. Once processes have been documented, then the organization can think about optimizing and eventually automating the processes. Optimization is done through a combination of manual analysis as well as automated simulation.

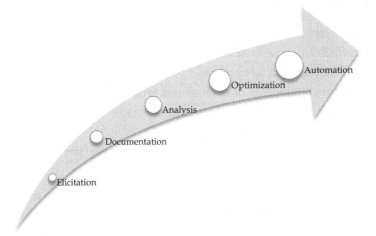

FIGURE 1-1. BUSINESS PROCESS MODELING STEPS

Aside from modeling business processes, an organization may also choose to model other activities. Hence, going forward we will use the more generic term *process modeling* as the techniques and principles described in this book apply to any kind of activity modeling, not just business processes.

The goal of this book is the exploration of the *art* of process elicitation, documentation, visual modeling, and analysis. We will look at the different techniques that are commonly in use, when to apply these techniques, and their trade-offs. Each of them will be supported with examples drawn from actual consulting engagements and process modeling efforts.

Modeling is subjective and requires not only precise "engineering" skills but also subtle human relations talent. Articulating, documenting, analyzing, and communicating processes is as much of an art as it is science and engineering. While many of the techniques can be taught, their application is much more imprecise. It is the goal of this book to illustrate this art in the context of a meticulous "engineering" framework and provide the practicing as well as novice business analyst with a set of principles they can immediately apply and as a result increase the quality of their work.

Case Study

The examples are drawn from a single case: a student aid organization. The mission of the organization is to provide micro loans or grants to students during their matriculation at college. The loans or grants are intended to provide bridge financing and generally are in the range of $100 - $1,000. The organization is required to track loans, recipients, payments, and funding sources. In addition, the organization must issue bills and generate various management reports. We will explore the business processes surrounding that organization with the goal that some of the processes will be partially automated using a variety of custom and off-the-shelf information systems.

Process and Workflow Modeling

The Business Analysis Body of Knowledge (*BABOK*) explains that "a process model is a visual representation of the sequential flow and control logic of a set of related activities or actions. Process modeling is used to obtain a graphical representation of a current or future process within an organization. A model may be used at its highest level to obtain a general understanding of a process or at a lower level as a basis for simulation so that the process can be made as efficient as possible."[1]

A workflow model is the visualization of the distribution of processes across responsible parties. The construction of visual workflow models is an essential technique that the business analyst needs to master. The *BABOK* defines a workflow model as "a visual representation of the flow of work in a business area. Workflow models are used to

---

[1] IIBA *BABOK* 2.0, Section 9.21

document how work processes are carried out, and to find opportunities for process improvement."

Process modeling encompasses system process modeling, business process modeling, and workflow modeling. Business processes are an essential component of the Business Architecture and ought to be maintained by the business.

Process Modeling Notations

The *BABOK* does not prescribe a specific notation for workflow models, although the use of a standard notation is suggested. During the past decade, the Unified Modeling Language (*UML*) has emerged as a *de facto* industry standard for the visual representation of analysis and design artifacts. Therefore, it is essential for the practicing business analyst to understand how workflow models can be represented in UML.

BPMN emerged as an alternative standard at about the same time as UML. BPMN is short for Business Process Modeling Notation. Its expressive power is virtually identical to UML, although its visual symbols look a bit different. However, BPMN is purely for process modeling. It does not offer any support for modeling data, deliverables, roles, organizations, lifecycle states, or systems. For that you will still need to use UML.

Both UML and BPMN are maintained by the Object Management Group[2], an industry consortium supported by virtually all major software and tool vendors. Its mission is the development and dissemination of modeling, execution, and middleware standards.

As an alternative to UML and BPMN, many business analyst use the classic flowchart notion developed in the early 1970's. This notation is somewhat outdated and does not provide the richness of either UML or BPMN.

Why Build Models?

Models, particularly visual ones, are developed in order to:

- document a business or some other process

---

[2] For more information on the OMG, visit www.omg.org.

- identify weaknesses in the process
- evaluate improvements to the process
- communicate business logic to stakeholders
- aid in the automation of processes through information systems
- gain consensus among stakeholders
- facilitate on-boarding of new employees
- meet regulatory compliance needs

Role of the Business Analyst

The business analyst has emerged as one of the most critical roles on information system and process improvement projects. In that role, the business analyst is responsible for gathering, analyzing, documenting, and communicating requirements and assuring that the final product meets the requirements and desired business objectives. This liaison role is also known as an Information System Analyst, System Analyst, Business Systems Analyst, or Business Architect.

Commonly, the business analyst is asked to carry out the following functions:

- Determine requirements activities
- Gather, analyze, and document requirements
- Communicate and validate requirements
- Manage changes to requirements
- Prepare feasibility studies

The successful business analyst needs a broad set of skills. He needs a solid understanding of requirements modeling, requirements analysis & documentation, database design, software design, project planning, and financial feasibility analysis. In addition, he must have knowledge of the business domain and the business environment. Finally, to be effective, he must know how to conduct interviews, manage meetings, write reports, and think critically.

Business Analysis Body of Knowledge

The Business Analysis Body of Knowledge (*BABOK* for short) is a guide to the different knowledge areas and associated activities and techniques that a practicing business analyst should master. The *BABOK* is published by the International Institute of Business

Analysis (*IIBA*). The *IIBA* also provides professional certification for senior business analysis through the Certified Business Analysis Professional (*CBAP*) designation[3].

While the *BABOK* is not a prescribed analysis methodology, it recognizes seven essential knowledge areas including business analysis planning and monitoring, elicitation, requirements management and communication, enterprise analysis, requirements analysis, solution assessment and validation, and underlying competencies such as leadership, problem solving, and communication skills (Figure 1-2.)

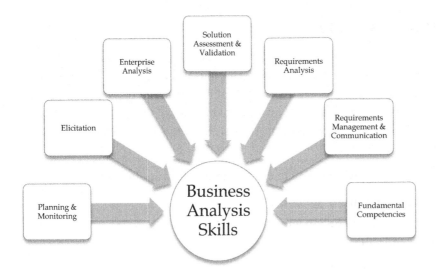

FIGURE 1-2. BUSINESS ANALYSIS KNOWLEDGE AREAS

Modeling versus Analysis

Process Modeling is the representation of the essential activities that make up some task whereas *Process Analysis* is the act of taking a process and analyzing it for shortcomings, *e.g.*, bottlenecks, inefficiencies, cost, resource consumption, and so forth. Therefore,

---

[3] See www.theiiba.org for more information on certification and the *BABOK*.

having a complete and correct process model is a prerequisite to meaningful process analysis.

In this book, we will focus principally on process modeling, *i.e.*, the capturing, articulation, and documentation of processes, rather than analysis. Analysis (and eventually optimization) is generally done by operations management specialists. However, one area where business analysts are often involved is process re-engineering driven by automation where a process needs to be changed to suit some new system or to remove some obvious inefficiencies before the process is automated through a system.

Modeling versus Drawing

Modeling imposes structure and is not simply a drawing. Proper modeling imposes a certain intellectual rigor on the artifacts being created and visually represented. This is one of the reasons why the use of a standard visual modeling language is critical. Both UML and BPMN contain modeling elements with specific semantic properties. It forces the business analyst to be precise. Too often, business analysts sketch workflow models that use icons incorrectly which can lead to misinterpreted and imprecise models. If the models are used for system construction then the resulting solution will necessarily be inadequate or perhaps completely wrong. Consequently, resources are wasted and system work must be redone at great expense.

The business analyst must have a solid understanding of the modeling languages being used to represent processes. While visual languages such as UML and BPMN are not difficult to apply, they do take time to learn. During validation, it may be necessary that the business analyst interpret diagrams when stakeholders and subject matter experts may not fully understand the symbology of the visual language. Business analysts should be prepared to provide short guides to their stakeholders, kind of like a Rosetta Stone for process modeling.

Process Modeling Approach

Process modeling should be done in a methodical manner so as to maximize its likelihood of success. A successful business process modeling effort results in an accurate model that is concisely represented in both visual and textual artifacts. The model reflects the actual business practices and procedures and can be considered a standard.

Business Architecture

Process models are built around four elements of the overall business architecture:

Resources. This includes people, materials, information (data), and systems. Resources are consumed, produced, or transformed by a process.

Results. The outcome or deliverables of the process that provide value to the business. Results can be a product or a service, but every process must have a result.

Rules. The process activities are governed by internal policies and guidelines or external regulations and laws. The rules define how the business must operate and therefore are an important constraint on activities within a process.

Events. A trigger for the initiation or termination of a process or some activity within a process. Events can be internal or external to the organization.

Processes describe how resources are used and transformed to achieve a set of results within the constraints of the applicable rules.

Perspective

Process models represent either the current state ("*as-is*") or the future state ("*to-be*"). Models should be created from a particular perspective and should not mix current and future state.

Process Modeling Tools

Processes must be stored, shared, and periodically updated. For that it is best to use a process management tool. Table 1-1 lists process management and modeling tools.

TABLE 1-1. PROCESS MODELING TOOLS

Tool	Vendor	BPMN	UML	Collaboration	Simulation	Data Modeling	Impact Analysis	Cost
Business Manager	Savvion	Yes	No	Yes	Yes	No	Yes	$$$
Enterprise Architect	Sparx	Yes	Yes	No	No	Yes	No	$
Visual Architect	Visual Paradigm	Yes	Yes	Yes	No	Yes	Yes	$

Tool	Vendor	BPMN	UML	Collaboration	Simulation	Data Modeling	Impact Analysis	Cost
ProVision BPM	MetaStorm	Yes	No	Yes	Yes	No	Yes	$$$
Process Modeler	BizAgi	Yes	No	Yes	Yes	No	No	Free
Process Maker	Colosa	Yes	No	No	No	No	No	Free

Summary

- Articulating business processes is a necessary precursor to automation
- Process models are constructed in a methodical manner and are presented in a standard notation
- UML and BPMN are the two most commonly used standard notations for process visualization, although the classic flowchart method is still in common use

2   *PROMAP MODELING FRAMEWORK*

Chapter Objectives

- Define the components of a process model
- Understand the *PROMAP* process modeling methodology
- Learn about the different diagrams and models that need to be created

A process model is more than a simple flowchart. It is a collection of interrelated artifacts that explain the process within the context of the business architecture. The business architecture contains definitions of the roles in the organization, resources, events, goals, systems, rules, and workflows. Processes are connected to all of these and are thus at the heart of the business architecture.

In fact every process:

- has an explicit and measurable goal
- takes specific inputs, generally in the form of information
- produces specific outputs, generally in the form of new or transformed information
- uses resources, including people, materials, and systems
- consists of a collection of ordered activities
- affects multiple organizational units or individuals
- produces a product or service of value to an internal or external stakeholder

Consequently, we need to model all of the above and not just draw a flowchart or workflow diagram.

Methodology

Analysis in general and process modeling in particular, must be done methodically and purposefully. Following a methodology allows the practitioner to focus on the actual work rather than worrying about what they should be doing next and whether they might be forgetting something. The methodology presented here is intended to be practical yet thorough. However, you should calibrate the methodology to your work environment, organizational culture, size of the modeling effort, and comfort with the techniques. Clearly, you don't need to do everything presented here for every process model you build. In fact, do the least amount of work possible, because everything beyond the minimum often does not add value. Of course, you need to do enough modeling work to assure that the project is not subject to undue risk.

PROMAP Framework

The approach detailed in this book is based on our practice-oriented approach called *PROMAP* – the *Pro*cess *M*odeling *Ap*proach. We have applied *PROMAP* on numerous projects with great success. Our clients value the progressive and structured nature of the approach.

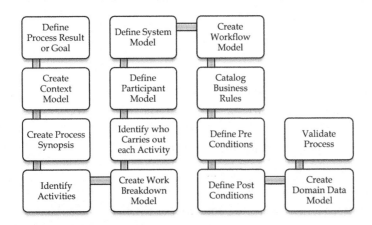

FIGURE 2-1. *PROMAP* FRAMEWORK FOR METHODICAL PROCESS MODELING

While the *PROMAP* framework appears to be sequential, it is decidedly not. It is unlikely that the steps will be carried out in exactly this order and it's very likely that you will need to revisit steps and enhance prior models and artifacts as you gain more insights into the process. Modeling is inherently iterative.

Process Model Components

A process model is a collection of several interrelated models, diagrams, and narratives. Overall, a process model consists of a process synopsis, context model, work breakdown model, participant model, system model, deliverable model, domain data model, workflow model, business rule catalog, and a process narrative (Figure 2-2.)

While a complex process might warrant the development of all of these components, a process model minimally consists of a process synopsis, a participant model, and a workflow model, although the preparation of a narrative is strongly suggested.

Any of the process model components represent either the current state (*"as-is"*) or the future state (*"to-be"*). Models, diagrams, and narratives should be created for a particular perspective and should not mix current and future state. Clearly label any process model components with the perspective.

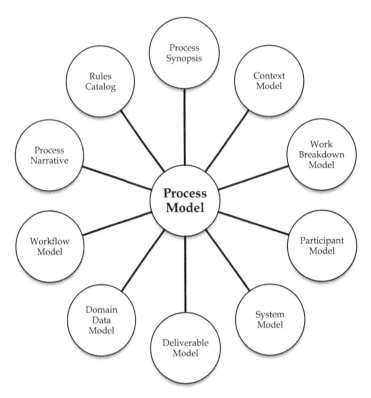

FIGURE 2-2. PROCESS MODEL COMPONENTS

The table below provides a summary of the process model components, their intent, and whether the component is considered to be necessary or optional. Naturally, the business analyst must decide whether building a particular component, be it a model, diagram, or narrative, clarifies the process. If a particular component does not help someone understand the process better, then it should not be created. After all, documentation must be maintained and therefore requires resources that perhaps could be spent better in other ways. Always weigh the value of the document against the cost of creating and maintaining it. Only if it has a positive cost-benefit should you write the document.

TABLE 2-1. PROCESS MODEL COMPONENTS

Component	Type	Intent	Need
Process Synopsis	Diagram	Summarizes participants, inputs, outputs, triggering event, and result for a process	Required

Context Model	Diagram	Summarizes participants and their information inflows and outflows for a process	Optional
Work Breakdown Model	Diagram	Shows the hierarchical decomposition of the process into activities and sub-activities	Suggested
Participant Model	Diagram + Matrix	Describes the profile of all process participants and shows their relationships	Required
System Model	Diagram + Matrix	Describes the profile of all systems and shows their relationships	Suggested
Deliverable Model	Matrix	Describes the results produced by the process	Suggested
Domain Data Model	Diagram + Matrix	Describes the information produced or consumed by a process and shows the relationships between objects	Suggested
Workflow Model	Diagram	Describes the sequence of activities that make up a process	Required
Process Narrative	Narrative	Describes a process and its results in text	Suggested
Rules Catalog	Narrative + Matrix	List of business rules and regulations that constrain the process activities	Suggested

The visual models are constructed as either UML or BPMN diagrams. Table 2-2 shows the model component and the UML or BPMN diagram that is used to represent it. As has been stated before, BPMN only supports the workflow model. Neither UML nor BPMN contain any support for text narratives of the process procedures.

TABLE 2-2. PROCESS MODEL COMPONENTS REPRESENTATION IN UML AND BPMN

Process Model Component	UML Diagram	BPMN Diagram
Process Synopsis	Composite Structure Diagram	N/A
Context Model	Composite Structure Diagram	N/A
Work Breakdown Model	Class Diagram	N/A
System Model	Deployment Diagram	N/A
Participant Model	Use Case Diagram	N/A
Deliverable Model	Class Diagram	N/A
Domain Data Model	Class Diagram	N/A

Workflow Model	Activity Diagram	Workflow Diagram
Process Narrative	N/A	N/A
Rules Catalog	N/A	N/A

Summary

- Modeling and diagramming is an iterative process
- The *PROMAP* framework is based on a collection of interrelated artifacts that align with the overall business architecture

3   *PROCESS ELICITATION*

Chapter Objectives

- Learn how to elicit the steps of a process
- Use brainstorming, interviewing, document analysis, and observation to find the process steps
- Apply mind mapping and context diagramming to process discovery
- Use statistical work sampling to efficiently find process variations

Elicitation is the act of discovering facts from the process participants and business domain experts. It is essentially a fact finding mission where the insights of business users, process participants, and domain experts are uncovered. Elicitation requires a significant amount of personal interaction and collaboration between the business analyst and the knowledge holders.

There are a number of commonly used process elicitation and fact discovery techniques available, including brainstorming, interviewing, document analysis, and observation (job shadowing).

All elicitation sessions must be held as collaborative sessions, ideally as face-to-face meetings. When direct contact with the process experts is not possible, then video conferencing, online conferencing, or telephone conversations can be substituted, although these communication modes are not nearly as efficient as direct interaction.

Elicitation Goals

Elicitation should focus on discovering the following facts about each process:

- Result or outcome of the process. Each process must produce some deliverable or carry out some service, *e.g.*, "disbursement" or "loan decision".

- Unique name of the process, *e.g.*, "render loan decision".
- Start event of the process, *i.e.*, the trigger that initiates the execution of the process, *e.g.*, "loan application received" or "payment received".
- People and information systems that participate in the process or that carry out activities within the process.
- Materials needed by the people or systems to carry out the activities. Materials can be tangible objects or intangible data stored in an information system.
- Activities that produce the result of the process. The activities may be higher level and are often broken down further.
- Sequencing of the activities.
- Rules that govern the execution of activities within the process. These are generally business rules but may also be system or regulatory constraints.
- Any pre-conditions that must be satisfied for the process to successfully complete, *e.g.*, "loan not paid off" or "student is matriculated". If any of these conditions are not true, then the process cannot produce its result.
- Any post-conditions that will be true upon successful completion of the process, *e.g.*, "loan payment recorded", "principal balance reduced", or "payment history updated".

Recording Discoveries

Any insights or discoveries made during elicitation sessions need to be recorded. There are a number of approaches to recording facts:

- Write discoveries on index cards or sticky notes and pin them to a whiteboard, wall, or on top of a table. Index cards are particularly useful because they can be moved around.
- Use whiteboards or flipcharts to record your discoveries.
- Record the elicitation session so that details can be revisited later. Be sure to check with the session participants whether they agree to being recorded. Keep in mind that they may not be as honest if they know they are being recorded.
- Use computer-based visual modeling tools to record process insights. While this approach generally yields the cleanest output it is often the least effective as there is often too much of a focus on the workings of the tool rather than the interaction between the business analyst and the stakeholders.

The use of tangibles such as index cards or sticky notes is encouraged during elicitation. Give session participants their own pen to write and let them get involved. Engaged participants contribute better insights and they understand that they own the process. Tangibles on walls or tables can also be moved around more easily and process steps can be more easily grouped and ordered.

While process modeling tools aren't bad *per se*, they do make the session participants more passive, though. Someone has to "drive the tool" which means that the others are now passive observers which likely means that they will feel less engaged and may become distracted.

Brainstorming

Brainstorming is used to discover process details through informal group sessions. Such sessions must be moderated by a good facilitator to be successful. Facilitation aids such as mind mapping or context diagramming are commonly employed during brainstorming sessions to increase their efficacy. Brainstorming is almost always followed up with more in-depth process elicitation techniques such as interviewing or observation.

Brainstorming Process

Start a brainstorming session by defining the process to be explored. Then ask the participants to identify the goal of the process. Next, ask them to brainstorm all of the activities (tasks) that need to be accomplished to achieve the goal of the process. Write the activities on index cards and place them on a large table surface or stick them to a wall. Then for each identified activity, ask the session participants whether this particular task requires some other activity to have been done beforehand. Sort the activities in order of execution and place the index cards in order on the table or wall. Finally, group the activities into themes, *i.e.*, activities that are logically cohesive. This is one of the primary reasons why index cards work better compared to whiteboarding or a visual modeling with a computer-based tool.

Once the activities have been ordered, identify any assumptions that were made and record those assumptions as pre-conditions. Identify any inputs or outputs that are being consumed or produced by each work task. That means any materials, supplies, systems, or data that is needed by each worker to perform the task. As you go through this effort, record any rules that need to be observed.

Finally, for each task ask the session participants who is expected to carry out the task – those are the workers. Create a separate lane for each worker and place the index card for the task into that worker's lane.

If you see that a session participant is dominating the discussion or that some participants feel intimidated by others, have the participants write their ideas anonymously on index cards and then pin them up for discussions. Read them out loud and debate them.

Once the process has been substantially elicited, then the information is recorded in a narrative and eventually in a formal UML or BPMN workflow model.

Mind Mapping

Mind mapping is a great technique for visualizing process steps and their relationships. The concept of mind mapping has been around for thousands of years, but really came into use during the 1950's when semantic networks were starting to be applied to modeling how the brain organizes information. A mind map is very similar to a concept map.

Mind maps are created around a single idea placed at the center of the diagram. Associated or related ideas are then connected to the central idea without regard to hierarchy or importance. They can also be used to clarify an idea or organize a complex problem.

Mind mapping software can be used to effectively map ideas and concepts spatially during brainstorming sessions. Some mind mapping tools are *MindMapper*, *MindManager*, *Freemind* (open source), and *Visual Mind*, among many others.

Figure 3-1 shows an example mind map for a brainstorming session for an "online loan application" process[4]. The items on the right are the process steps with brainstormed notes and associated rules, while the items on the left are conditions and constraints.

Once the mind map is completed, the results are then recorded in a narrative and eventually in a more formal workflow model using a visual modeling tool and a standard notation such as UML or BPMN.

---

[4] Drawn using the open source and free *FreeMind* tool.

FIGURE 3-1. PROCESS BRAINSTORMING RESULTS EXPRESSED IN A MIND MAP

Context Diagramming

Another diagram often used during brainstorming sessions is the context diagram. The context diagram is essentially a Level 0 data flow diagram (DFD) illustrating a process and the participants (also called *workers* or *actors* by some) that are involved in it. The diagram focuses only on information inflows and outflows between the external entities (external or internal process participants) and the process. A context diagram used in information system engineering is called a system context diagram, while a context diagram used for business process modeling is called a process context diagram. Process context diagrams are an important component of the overall process model and will be explored in more detail in a later chapter.

There are several notations in use, although the most common notation places the process under investigation as a circle at the center of the diagram with the external entities – drawn as rectangles – surrounding it (see Figure 3-2.) Arrows indicate information inflows or outflows. The flows generally represent data, objects, or materials. The data inflows and outflows are purposely not described in detail. The diagram is meant to be a high-level analysis and scoping diagram and not a detailed design diagram.

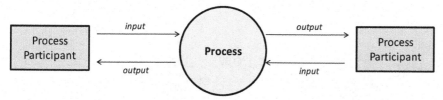

FIGURE 3-2. CONTEXT DIAGRAMMING NOTATION

As an alternative, a context diagram can be constructed in a modified diagram of the Unified Modeling Language. This is explained in more detail in a subsequent chapter.

Decomposition

Processes can be high-level or detailed. If a process has more than 7-10 steps, build a hierarchy where the high-level process is 7-10 steps and complex steps are described in more detail separately. Use a work breakdown model to illustrate the hierarchy of the process. See Chapter 6 for more details on the work breakdown model.

Interviews

Interviews are a direct interaction (face to face or via technology such as telephone, online meeting, or video) between the business analyst and the process experts. Interviewing is probably the most widely practiced elicitation technique and is often used in conjunction with observation and after initial brainstorming sessions.

Interviews are used to find, verify, and elaborate facts as well as identify process steps and solicit ideas, opinions, and preferences. They are also used to generate enthusiasm about a process mapping effort and to get stakeholders engaged.

Ideally, interviews are conducted as face-to-face sessions lasting about 30 minutes to an hour. Longer interviews are discouraged as participants tire after about 45 minutes. If a face-to-face meeting is not feasible due to time or geographical constraints, then a telephone or online video conference can be substituted (see Figure 3-3 for a partial list of online meeting tools).

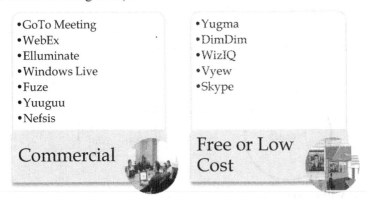

- GoTo Meeting
- WebEx
- Elluminate
- Windows Live
- Fuze
- Yuuguu
- Nefsis

Commercial

- Yugma
- DimDim
- WizIQ
- Vyew
- Skype

Free or Low Cost

FIGURE 3-3. LIST OF ONLINE MEETING TOOLS

Interviewing Guidelines

Initially, an unstructured interview – conducted similarly to a brainstorming session with few, if any, specific questions – may be appropriate, but then a more structured interview with a specific set of questions should be used.

You can start by asking open-ended questions requiring a free form response but then follow-up with closed-ended questions where you expect the interviewee to pick a response from a list of specific choices or respond with short and direct answers.

Gauging a person's communication style might be beneficial. Find out if the person is an effusive talker or needs encouragement and specific questions to reveal facts. Adjust your questioning accordingly.

Interact with interviewees to have them respond freely and openly, but probe for more feedback. Observe nonverbal communication; it can reveal a great deal about a participant's attitude toward the project or line of questioning.

Interviews are an effective although time-consuming way to get facts. Their success is highly dependent on the business analyst's human relations skills. Make sure that you avoid loaded or leading questions that might reveal your own bias. Don't include your opinion as part of the question. Use clear and concise language and avoid long or complex questions. Avoid using technical jargon that might not be understood by your business stakeholders.

In the interview listen carefully, maintain control of the interview, ask probing and follow-up questions, and make sure that you understand what the interviewee is saying. Repeat what they are saying and practice active listening. You should listen more than talk.

Observe their mannerisms and nonverbal communication; it might reveal a lot about how they feel about the project, you, or your questions. Above all, be patient, keep the interviewee at ease, and maintain self-control. Be sure that you finish on time – stick to your deadlines; after all, your stakeholders may have another commitment right after your interview; value their time.

When possible bring a scribe to take notes or record the meeting using tools such as *LiveScribe*, *OneNote* or *Audacity* – these tools allow archiving and searching of the recording for keywords later. Of course, ask for permission first before you record; it might be against an organization's policies.

Interview Preparation

Prepare for the interview by writing down your agenda in an interview guide; use the guide in Figure 3-4 as a template. Record the answers to your questions in the log section. The guide can be a printed form or completed on a computer using a word processor or some other tool. Keep in mind that typing while someone is speaking is often perceived as distracting.

Always ask who else you should be speaking to when you conclude an interview; this reduces the likelihood that you forget to consult an important stakeholder.

Interviewer:	Mark Solenski	
Interviewee(s) Date & Time: Location: Purpose:	Moira Davis, Jeff Marino 12/03/09 at 10am LM-603B Understand payment recording process and necessary tracking data	
Allotted Time	_Question or Interview Goal_	_Response/Notes_
1 to 2 min.	Open interview: • Introductions • State goal of interview session	
5 min.	**Question 1** Which payments need to be tagged as past due and routed to A/R immediately for priority processing?	
30 min.	**Question 2** Can you briefly describe the steps you go through to record a payment for a loan after you have received a check?	
10 min.	**Question 3** Can you briefly describe which payment statuses (states) you need to know about and how these are used	

	by the business?	
1 min.	**Question 4** *Who else do you think I should be talking to?*	
<u>*Total Time*</u>: 50 min.		
Notes:		

FIGURE 3-4. INTERVIEW PREPARATION GUIDE

Document Analysis

Document analysis is an inspection of existing documentation including organization charts, operating procedures, training manuals, flowcharts and other process maps, and any other documents that describe the process or provide context and background to the analysis effort.

You will often find that once you visualize a written procedure that you discover oversights, flaws, and inconsistencies. Bring them to the attention of the business and use that to help the business understand the value of mapping processes visually.

Observation

Observation is a fact-finding technique in which the business analyst either participates in or watches a person perform activities to learn about the process. This technique is also known as job shadowing.

Observations can be active or passive. In an active observation, the business analyst asks questions, probes for details, and perhaps even participates in the process. In a passive observation, the business analyst does not interact with the person who is being observed; ideally, the person does not even know they are being observed, although that's often difficult to do in practice.

If a process or an activity has variations and is done differently at different points in time, then using work sampling – observations taken at random intervals – is a great way to cut down on the overall observation time. Use the sampling procedure presented below to help determine how many work periods you should observe to get an understanding of the variations in a process.

Figure 3-5 summarizes the benefits and challenges of the observation technique. Overall, observation is a great way to see how work is actually done rather than how stakeholders describe the process in interviews, although when observed some stakeholders may not do the work as they normally do – they may do it "by the book" and it's hard to see what they actually do when the business analyst is not around.

Benefits	Challenges
• Actually see how work is done rather than how people describe the work in an interview or in an operating procedure • Complex tasks are easier to understand • Relatively inexpensive to conduct • Ability to take measurements of time needed or materials used • Easier to identify hand-offs between multiple parties	• People may perform process differently when being observed • Work observed may not be representative of normal conditions • Timing can be inconvenient • Interruptions can throw off time measurements • Some tasks not always performed the same way • Different people may perform the same task differently

FIGURE 3-5. BENEFITS AND CHALLENGES OF OBSERVATION

A list of pros and cons of active and passive observation are summarized in the table below.

TABLE 3-1. PROS AND CONS OF ACTIVE AND PASSIVE OBSERVATION

	Pros	Cons
Active	Better understanding through hands-on experience Questions answered immediately, thereby minimizing requirements gathering time	Might be uncomfortable for participant Won't know how long process takes Inadvertent change of process More time needed to capture ideas and information
Passive	Accurate picture of how a process is done Understanding of how long the process takes to carry out	Unanswered questions require follow-up Can't ask for explanations

Work Sampling

It is unlikely that all variations of a process can be observed. For instance, what if you observe a call center for a day? Do you think that you will be able to observe all types of incoming calls and the accompanying process variations? Probably not! To increase the likelihood of observing all process variations, we need to increase our observation time, although that could be logistically difficult to accomplish. You probably don't have the time or the resources.

Alternatively, the process could be sampled. To do that, we break the observation period into smaller intervals and then have different people observe at different times. For instance, a call center process observation might be done as follows. Suppose that we have two weeks to do the observation. If we know that a typical call takes 10 minutes on average, then we can divide the two weeks into 10 minute chunks and randomly observe a sample of 10 minute chunks.

The question then is: How many sample periods must be observed to have a high degree of confidence that all process variations have been encountered?

Using statistical sampling theory and assuming a normal distribution of the special cases, the size of the sample can be estimated as follows[5]:

$$n = \sigma^2 \left(\frac{Z_{\alpha/2}}{\alpha} \right)^2$$

where:

σ^2 is the variance in the sample

α is the acceptable level of error

Z is the certainty factor for level $\alpha/2$ from table of Z scores (see Table 3-2 for select values)

---

[5] For a derivation of this formula consult any statistics book. It is an estimation of the sample size given a particular confidence interval and a known standard deviation.

The variance can be calculated from the probability that any given sample is a special case. Specifically,

$$\sigma^2 = pq = p(1-p)$$

If we do not know p we must assume that $p = 0.5$ which yields a variance of $p(1-p) = 0.25$.

Let's take a look at the example of the call center again. Suppose that you have been asked to analyze and re-engineer the incoming call handling process for a new call center management system. The new process is replacing an existing process. The old process has many variations and "odd cases" and you want to make sure that you are aware of all the exceptions as few of them are presently documented. You ask the call center technicians to estimate how many calls they get per week and how many of those are "special". Suppose that they tell you that they get about 200 calls per week and about 40 of them are "special". This means that there's an empirically derived probability that about 40/200 are special ($p = 0.2$.) You would like to know how many calls you would have to observe to be 90% certain (*alpha* or $\alpha = 0.1$ equivalent to a 10% acceptable error) that you have encountered all of the special situations. Here are the calculations for the sample size, *i.e.*, how many calls you need to observe:

$p = 0.2$ and $\alpha = 0.1$, $Z_{\alpha/2} = 1.645$ (Z score for $\alpha/2$ for a normal distribution from Table 3-2)

Therefore,

$$n = 0.2(1-0.2)\left(\frac{1.645}{0.1}\right)^2 \approx 30$$

That means that we should observe about 30 calls picked at random. It is important that the samples be selected at random. One way to do this is to write a computer program that generates 30 random observation time slots and then the business analyst observes calls during that time period. Perhaps if the calls were previously recorded then you could randomly listen to 30 recordings.

TABLE 3-2. TABLE OF SELECTED _Z_ SCORES FOR SAMPLE ESTIMATION

Desired Confidence	Matching $Z_{a/2}$ Score
99% ($\alpha = 0.01$)	2.576
95% ($\alpha = 0.05$)	1.960
90% ($\alpha = 0.10$)	1.645
80% ($\alpha = 0.20$)	1.281

Summary

- Elicitation can be done through informal brainstorming, formal interviewing, active or passive observation, and document analysis
- Mind mapping is a convenient way to break down process steps during initial brainstorming sessions
- Context diagramming can help elevate the discussion during elicitation sessions
- Random work sampling is used to find process variations without long and continuous observation

4 PROCESS CONTEXT AND SYNOPSIS

Chapter Objectives

- Summarize the process at a high level
- Construct context diagrams and process synopsis diagrams
- Learn about business use case diagrams

A process summary graphically depicts the process and the organizational roles and systems that participate in the process as well as information flows into and out of the process. There are three diagrams available to summarize the overall process: the process context diagram, the process synopsis, and the business use case diagram.

The process context diagram is similar in intent to a system context diagram: show information inflows and outflows. The difference is that a system context diagram shows a system and inflows and outflows to and from external entities that are connected to the system. A process context diagram, on the other hand, shows inputs and outputs to a process from process participants.

Similarly, the process synopsis also shows inputs and outputs, but not who provides them. The synopsis also depicts the triggering event and the result of the process along with the process participants. Both diagrams provide a high-level summary view of the process and either or both can be constructed depending on need.

The business use case diagram shows the least detail of the three. It only shows the process and its participants, but no information flows or other pertinent process information.

While it is often helpful to begin with these summary models at the outset of the modeling effort, some of the information might not be known until later.

Process Context Diagram

While the process diagram is not one of the standard UML diagrams, a composite structure diagram[6] can be used for that purpose. The process is depicted as a *collaboration* while the process participants are illustrated as business actors. Figure 4-1 shows the basic process context diagram structure.

If we wish to model the process context more precisely, we can use the business actor symbol for external process participants and the internal business worker symbol for process participants that are internal to the organization and that carry out the process. Figure 4-2 illustrates the UML symbols for that situation.

The final elaboration is presented in Figure 4-3. It contains internal and external participants as well as information inflows and outflows. Note that we now use directed dashed lines to connect the participants to the process so that we can distinguish between inflows and outflows. The directional lines have the stereotype *«flow»* in order to differentiate them from a UML dependency. While you may not want to tag your flow lines with that stereotype when quickly sketching the diagram on a whiteboard, it is important when using a UML modeling tool. The UML constructs are summarized in Table 4-1.

FIGURE 4-1. BASIC PROCESS CONTEXT DIAGRAM IN UML

---

[6] A *collaboration* in UML 2 is a set of cooperating roles and their connectors. It is principally used to illustrate a specific task or some functionality. The collaborating roles and their relationships are depicted in a *composite structure diagram*.

FIGURE 4-2. BASIC PROCESS CONTEXT DIAGRAM WITH INTERNAL AND EXTERNAL PARTICIPANTS

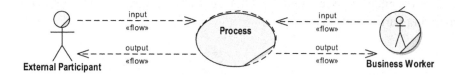

FIGURE 4-3. ELABORATE PROCESS DIAGRAM WITH INFORMATION FLOWS

The diagram in Figure 4-4 is an example of an elaborate process context diagram for the process "Provide Short-Term Funding" of our case study.

Conversations with the business experts revealed that the process involves three participants: the student who is requesting funding, the loan administrator who processes the application, and the officer who approves the application. Furthermore, we understand that students fill out an application and provide background information about themselves. The loan administrator reviews the application and the officer approves it. It is likely that additional data flows will become apparent during subsequent analysis.

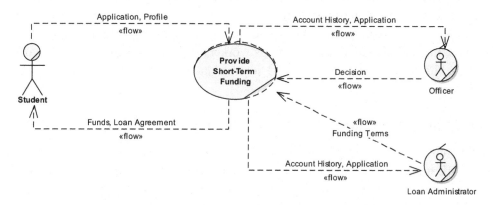

FIGURE 4-4. EXAMPLE: ELABORATE PROCESS CONTEXT DIAGRAM IN UML

Business Use Case Diagram

An alternative to the process context diagram is the business use case diagram of UML. A business use case is a narrative description of a business process expressed as a use case. The business use case diagram is a convenient summary of the participants in the business use case without any description of information flows. It is a less detailed diagram, but can be useful during early elicitation, particularly if stakeholders are familiar with use case analysis. See Figure 4-5 for an example of a business use case diagram summarizing participants in a process.

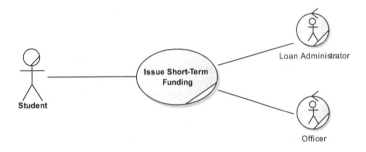

FIGURE 4-5. UML BUSINESS USE CASE DIAGRAM

Note that the symbols for business use case diagrams are somewhat different from traditional system use case diagrams. To visually distinguish a system use case from a business use case, the business use case symbol has a line through it. The same is true for an actor. Actors represent participants in the business use case. Like the other diagrams that involve process participants, we can differentiate between external and internal participants. Internal participants are business workers and have a different UML symbol than external business actors. See Table 4-1 for a summary of the different UML symbols and their semantics.

Classic Context Diagram

A classic context diagram can be used as an alternative to UML. This might be useful when a UML modeling tool is not available or there is concern that the symbols of UML are not easily understood by stakeholders even with explanation and guidance.

Ideally, modeling notations should not the mixed as that can lead to even more confusion. So, if you are going to use UML to model workflows, then you might as well use UML for all of the other process models.

A classic context diagram is actually a Level 0 Data Flow Diagram (DFD). One of the most common notations for diagramming DFDs was developed by Gane and Sarsen[7]. In this notation, the process name is written inside a circle at the center of the diagram, while process participants (called external entities) are depicted as rectangles. Lines with directional arrows are used to show data inflows and outflows. Figure 4-6 depicts the general symbols used in the Gane/Sarsen context diagram.

Figure 4-7 is a depiction of the previous process context model in the Gane/Sarsen notation.

FIGURE 4-6. CLASSIC CONTEXT DIAGRAM NOTATION

FIGURE 4-7. PROCESS CONTEXT MODEL IN CLASSIC GANE/SARSEN NOTATION

---

[7] Gane, C. and Sarson, T. "Structured Systems Analysis: Tools and Techniques", New York: IST, Inc., 1977.

Process Synopsis

The overall process structure is illustrated in a high-level summary diagram called the Process Synopsis. You should create one synopsis for every process that you are modeling. The synopsis is exactly what is says: a summary of the process elements. It shows the event that starts the process, all of the inputs (data and materials), any outputs that it generates or transforms, all of the participants (people and systems), and the final result of the process. The result must be some product or service.

The synopsis process diagram shown in Figure 4-8 is once again represented as a UML composite structure diagram since UML does not directly support a synopsis. If the UML composite structure diagram is not available in your modeling tool, a UML object diagram can also be used.

The inputs, outputs, and the result are all modeled as objects, while the triggering event is an event element. Participants as modeled as business actors and the process itself is a collaboration, although a business use case or a simple use case could also be used if the collaboration symbol is not supported by your tool. In fact, you can use any collection of symbols as long as you are consistent and the stakeholders clearly understand their semantics. Be sure to provide a legend or a guide to the notation you are using.

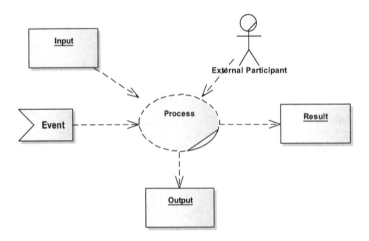

FIGURE 4-8. PROCESS SYNOPSIS DIAGRAM IN UML

As with the context diagrams, we can use business actors and business workers to visually differentiate between external and internal process participants along with control objects to indicate any systems that are used to carry out activities. A process synopsis showing business actors (external process participants), business workers (internal process participants), and systems is in Figure 4-9. Recall that internal and external refer to the organization that's executing the process.

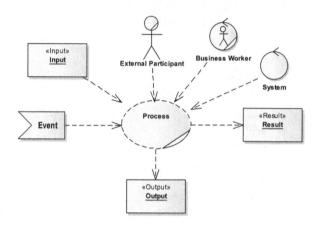

FIGURE 4-9. PROCESS SYNOPSIS WITH EXTERNAL AND INTERNAL PARTICIPANTS IN UML

Returning to our loan management system case, let's look at the process synopsis for the business process "Provide Short-Term Funding". Again, assuming that we have done some elicitation of the process details, we have made the following discoveries:

- the result of the process is giving funds (money) to a student
- inputs are the funding application and student profile
- outputs are the funds and a loan agreement
- the sole external participant is the student
- the internal participants are the loan administrator and the officer
- the event that triggers the process is the "request for funding"

Figure 4-10 illustrates the process synopsis for the process "Provide Short-Term Funding". Again, the synopsis is subject to revision as we make additional discoveries about the process. The construction is any process model is iterative and the various supporting models and diagrams will be revised continually during analysis.

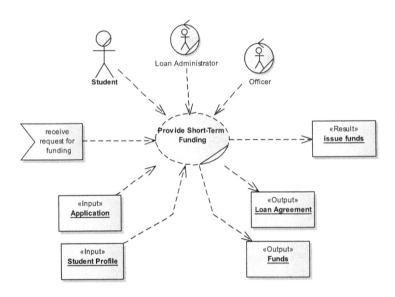

FIGURE 4-10. EXAMPLE PROCESS SYNOPSIS IN UML

Best Practice

So, which one of these diagrams do you use? Are they all the same? Well, not really. They all show something a bit different, although all of them depict the process "environment" if you will. I generally start during early elicitation sessions with a business use case diagram because I don't want to worry about information flows, input objects, results, and so forth. I generally move on to a work breakdown structure if the process is well understood. If the process is not well understood then an observation session or an activity brainstorming session are best. Once the process is a bit more established, I revisit the context diagram and add information flows. Sometimes, if we get stuck during activity elicitation, a context diagram can help "elevate" the discussion and get away from the "weeds". Although, once everything is done, I generally try to construct at least a process synopsis. It provides a high-level summary view of the process.

UML Symbol Digest

The UML symbols and their meaning are summarized in the table below. There are no equivalent symbols in BPMN as that notation does not support anything but workflow diagrams.

TABLE 4-1. UML SYMBOLS FOR PROCESS CONTEXT MODELING

Concept	UML Symbol	Meaning	Usage
Process	Process	Business or other process	Context Model Process Synopsis
Business Use Case	Business Use Case	A business process expressed as a use case	Business Use Case Diagram
External Participant (Business Actor)	External Participant	A participant in a process that is outside the organization executing the process	Context Diagram Process Synopsis Business Use Case Diagram
Internal Participant (Business Worker)	Business Worker	A participant in a process that is inside the organization executing the process	Context Diagram Process Synopsis Business Use Case Diagram
Participant (Generic Actor)	Participant	A generic participant in a process; can be internal or external. Used when internal and external participants are not to be distinguished	Context Diagram Process Synopsis Business Use Case Diagram
Internal System	System	A system that is used to partially or fully carry out an activity	Context Diagram Process Synopsis
Event	Event	A trigger that starts the process	Process Synopsis Workflow Diagram
Input	Input	An object that is consumed or transformed by the process	Process Synopsis

Concept	UML Symbol	Meaning	Usage
Output	Output	An object that is produced by the process	Process Synopsis
Result	Result	The result, goal, or outcome of the process	Process Synopsis
Connector	---------------	Connects a participant to a process	Context Diagram Process Synopsis
Connector	_____	Connects an actor to a business use case	Business Use Case Diagram
Information Flow	----«flow»---->	Shows an information (data) inflow or outflow	Context Diagram Process Synopsis

The detailed workflow diagramming constructs will be explained in more detail in a subsequent chapter.

Summary

- Modeling and diagramming is an iterative process
- Models are most commonly visualized in UML
- The context model summarizes the process participants and the information inflows and outflows
- The process synopsis summarizes the process participants, input and output objects, triggering event, and the overall process result
- UML composite structure diagrams are used to depict the process context and synopsis
- The process synopsis is the best high-level summary diagram

5   PROCESS NARRATIVES

Chapter Objectives

- Describe processes textually
- Construct a concise process narrative
- Learn how to identify process exceptions

Narratives are text documents that describe the process in words. They should be written concisely but accurately and must be accompanied by diagrams. Narratives are more easily understood if they are visualized with diagrams particularly a workflow model.

The business analyst has to decide how much narrative documentation is appropriate for some particular process modeling effort. As has been mentioned already, a business analyst should write the least amount of documentation necessary to communicate the process clearly and unambiguously. On an agile project, verbal communication is often substituted for written communication thus resulting is less overall written documentation.

Justify Documentation

When a business analyst creates a work product, be it a narrative, diagram, model, matrix, or other artifact, he or she should always ask:

- Why is this artifact needed?
- What purpose does the artifact serve?
- Who will need this artifact and what will they need it for?
- Is the artifact prepared in a manner that is useful to its ultimate consumer?

- Does the value of the artifact exceed the cost of creating and maintaining it?

Only produce what you need. Documentation and visual models take time to write and much of that effort does not produce value for the business. See the "Golden Rules" of business analysis below.

> **Rule 1**: It is the responsibility of the Business Analyst to communicate not to document.
>
> **Rule 2**: Adjust the amount of analysis and documentation that is prepared to a level that assures a full understanding of the discovery, but nothing more.

Elements of a Narrative

The process narrative is often the document of record for the process. While it is supported by a number of models and diagrams, it does in fact contain the majority of the process definition.

Although there is no industry standard for the narrative, the narrative document should follow a project-standard template. The template should minimally contain the elements listed in the table below.

TABLE 5-1. ELEMENTS OF A PROCESS NARRATIVE

Element	Description	Associated Artifact
Identifier	Unique identifier using format *PXXX* where *XXX* is a unique number	N/A
Name	Name of the process; should be a verb phrase.	N/A
Perspective	Either current state ("as-is") or future state ("to-be")	N/A
Trigger	Triggering event	Context Diagram Process Synopsis
Goal/Result	Outcome of the process	Process Synopsis
Participants	List of all internal and external process participants	Context Diagram Process Synopsis Workflow Diagram
Started By	Person, organization, event, or time that starts the process	Workflow Diagram

Element	Description	Associated Artifact
Pre-Conditions	Conditions that must be true in order for the process to succeed	Workflow Diagram
Post-Conditions	Conditions that will be true at the successful or unsuccessful conclusion of the process	Workflow Diagram
Actions	An ordered list of steps that describes the activities that will be carried out by the process participants to achieve the goal of the process	Workflow Diagram
Variations	A list of exceptions and alternate flows	Workflow Diagram
Rules	A numbered list of associated business rules	Rules Catalog

Writing the Narrative

The narrative contains the information discovered during the elicitation sessions, be it interviews, brainstorming workshops, observation, or document analysis.

When defining the process actions, focus initially on the normal or basic path through the process. Once the basic path has been defined, define exceptions or alternate flows for each step. Record the discoveries in the narrative and concurrently draw the various supporting artifacts, particularly the process synopsis, workflow model, and rules catalog.

The actions should be written in a *participant/action/object/goal* format:

> The [participant] [acts] [upon some object] [to achieve some goal].

For example:

> The student [*participant*] fills out [*acts*] a loan application [*upon some object*] to obtain funding [*to achieve some goal*].

Number the actions sequentially. When you encounter an exception or some variation in the process list the condition or event that causes the variation and document the variation separately. Number the variations sequentially and then refer to them in parenthesis from the basic actions that have the variations.

Clearly identify the boundaries of the process by starting with the action phrase:

> This process starts when [list the triggering event].

End each process narrative with the action phrase:

This process ends when [final action].

Best Practices for Process Modeling

Stakeholders often don't know their processes well. Asking for the "first step" may confuse them. A better approach might be to ask:

- *What happens during this process?*
- *What tasks do have to be accomplished to achieve the process goal?*
- *What does the process produce as its deliverable?*
- *Who participates in the process?*

Don't focus on the order of steps. Afterwards, for each step ask them:

- *What other step must be completed before this one can be done?*
- *Who carries out the activity?*
- *Does it always happen like this?*
- *When does this step get done differently?*

Now you are ordering the activities and you are starting to elicit the branches in the flow.

It's often much easier to define the pre- and post-conditions after you have investigated the basic and alternate flows.

Annotated Narrative

To illustrate how to write a narrative, let's take a look at the process "Provide Short-Term Funding" from the loan management system case. Figure 5-1below defines the process textually using a template containing the elements listed in Table 5-1.

Process Identifier:	BP001
Process Name:	Provide Short-Term Funding
Perspective:	Current State ("as-is")

Triggering Event:	Student asks for financial support
Goal:	Provide funding for a student either as a short-term loan or a grant
Participants:	Student; Loan Administrator; Officer; Treasurer
Started By:	Student
Pre-Conditions:	Student is matriculated at the College; Student has a satisfactory history of paying back loans; Funds are available for disbursement
Post-Conditions:	Student has received funds in the form of a check or cash; Student has signed a loan agreement if the funding was a loan
Actions:	1. This process starts when a student asks for funding. 2. The student fills out an application for funding. 3. The student submits the application. 4. The loan administrator marks the application with the current date. 5. The loan administrator checks the application for completeness and qualification. {V1;V2} 6. The loan administrator retrieves the funding history for the student. {V3} 7. The loan administrator interviews the student to determine the actual need for the funding request. 8. The loan administrator decides whether to grant the funding request if the request is for less than $250. {V4} 9. The loan administrator determines the funding type (loan or grant). 10. The loan administrator prepares a loan agreement for the student to sign. {V5} 11. The student signs the loan agreement. 12. The loan administrator routes the approval to the treasurer. 13. The treasurer issues the funds as one or more checks and/or cash the next business day. {V6} 14. The process ends when the student accepts the funds.

Variations:	V1. Application Not Complete:
	   1.1. Ask student to provide missing information.
	   1.2. Repeat Step 2
	V2. Student Does Not Qualify for Funding: {BR1;BR2}
	   2.1. Process terminates
	V3. No Funding History:
	   3.1. Create a profile for the student.
	   3.2. Resume at next step
	V4. Request Exceeds $250:
	   4.1. Route funding request to Officer.
	   4.2. The officer reviews applications and renders decision.
	   4.3. The officer informs the loan administrator of the decision.
	   4.4. Resume at next step
	V5. Grant Issued Instead of Loan:
	   5.1. Skip to Step 12
	V6. Cash Issued Instead of Check:
	   6.1. The student signs a receipt for the cash.

	6.2. The loan administrator gives the cash to the student.
	6.3. The loan administrator enters the disbursement into the petty cash log.
	6.4. Resume at Step 14
Business Rules:	BR1. Only matriculated students may obtain funding.
	BR2. Only students with a satisfactory loan re-payment history may be granted additional funding.
	BR3. An officer must approve any funding request in excess of $250.
	BR4. Funds can be disbursed as a combination of cash and multiple checks.
	BR5. There is a minimum waiting period of one business day before funds are disbursed.

FIGURE 5-1. ANNOTATED PROCESS NARRATIVE

Once the steps for the process have been elicited, ask the process experts what constraints, rules, or regulations must be observed for each step. Record these rules in a separate rule catalog or as part of the process narrative.

Summary

- Narratives are written for each process to provide details
- Narratives should be concise yet detailed and follow a standard template
- Narratives are supported by workflow models and other diagrams

6   WORK BREAKDOWN MODEL

Chapter Objectives

- Identify process activities through hierarchical decomposition
- Construct a work breakdown structure

The work breakdown model is a hierarchical decomposition of the process into its activities. Complex activities are further broken down into sub-activities and those sub-activities are then decomposed again until there are only actions remaining that can be carried out by a single person in a relatively short amount of time.

The work breakdown model is very similar to a work breakdown structure (WBS) used in project management. It helps in clarifying the steps of a process and identifying the final actions that comprise the process.

Note that the work breakdown model is often developed during initial elicitation sessions and often before the process narrative. It is a technique that the business analyst needs to apply whenever it is most appropriate and will be most effective in getting the process definition.

Process Decomposition

The work breakdown is the result of a top-down decomposition of the process hierarchy. We can graphically express the hierarchy in a UML class diagram. BPMN does not have any support for work breakdown. Figure 6-1 illustrates the UML structure for a work breakdown model of a process. The icon with the rhombus at one end is a UML aggregation. It indicates that an activity is "composed of" other activities which is the essence of a work breakdown.

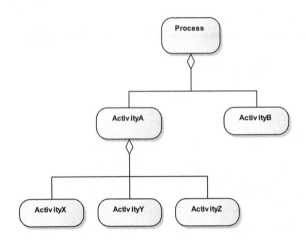

FIGURE 6-1. WORK BREAKDOWN MODEL IN UML

The activities described in the work breakdown model must be the same as the ones included in the workflow model. Make sure that the two models are consistent. Once again, modeling tools can greatly simplify or in many cases fully automate the task of synchronization.

The activities in the work breakdown model are not expected to be ordered in any way. In fact it is detrimental to the analysis process to focus on ordering the activities when constructing a work breakdown model. Defer sequencing of activities until the workflow modeling phase.

The work breakdown model is an excellent technique to apply during initial process elicitation sessions. It is more formal than the mind mapping technique that was previously introduced, but otherwise very similar in intent. The key is to get the stakeholders and process experts to focus on what needs to get done to achieve a goal and not so much how and by whom it gets done. The how and by-whom will be addressed during work flow modeling and when writing the process narrative.

Figure 6-2 shows a partial work breakdown structure for the business process "Provide Short-Term Funding" from the loan management system case. Incidentally, it is not unusual to break a large work breakdown model into several smaller ones.

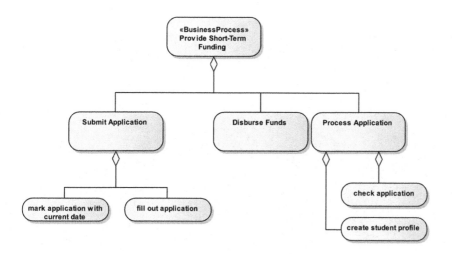

FIGURE 6-2. EXAMPLE OF A PARTIAL WORK BREAKDOWN MODEL

Summary

- Work breakdown models are a top-down decomposition of a process into constituent activities and their associated sub-activities
- The work breakdown model is a UML class diagram using aggregation as the relationship between activities and sub-activities
- Ordering of activities is not important when building a work breakdown model

7   *WORKFLOW MODELING*

Chapter Objectives

- Visualize the process through a workflow diagram
- Construct workflow diagrams in UML and BPMN with a focus on UML
- Learn advanced visualization and process definition techniques

The construction of workflow models is an essential technique that the business analyst needs to master. The *BABOK* defines a workflow model as "a visual representation of the flow of work in a business area. Workflow models are used to document how work processes are carried out, and to find opportunities for process improvement." The *BABOK* does not prescribe a specific notation for workflow models, although the use of a standard notation is suggested. For the past decade, the Unified Modeling Language (*UML*) and the Business Process Modeling Notation (*BPMN*) have emerged as *de facto* industry standards for the visual representation of analysis and design artifacts. Therefore, it is essential for the practicing analyst to understand how workflow models are visualized in UML and BPMN.

Recall that the graphical workflow model is supported by a detailed process narrative. There is necessarily overlap between these two documentation artifacts, but that is acceptable. Some insights are more easily conveyed in text while others are best described in a diagram.

The workflow model must describe either the current state ("as-is") or future state ("to-be") of a process and any diagram must be clearly marked with the perspective to avoid confusion.

This chapter shows both UML and BPMN workflow models, but the focus in on UML.

Workflow Model Elements

Regardless of the actual notation used, a workflow model minimally has the following elements:

- <u>Activities/Tasks</u>: steps of the process
- <u>Sequential flows</u>: direction of the sequence
- <u>Decision points</u>: mutually exclusive branches in the process
- <u>Parallel flows</u>: inclusive or concurrent branch points in the process
- <u>Swimlanes</u>: divisions of activities among participating actors
- <u>Roles</u>: actors participating in process
- <u>Terminals</u>: source and sinks of the process

Getting Started

Figure 7-1 summarizes the process and workflow modeling steps.

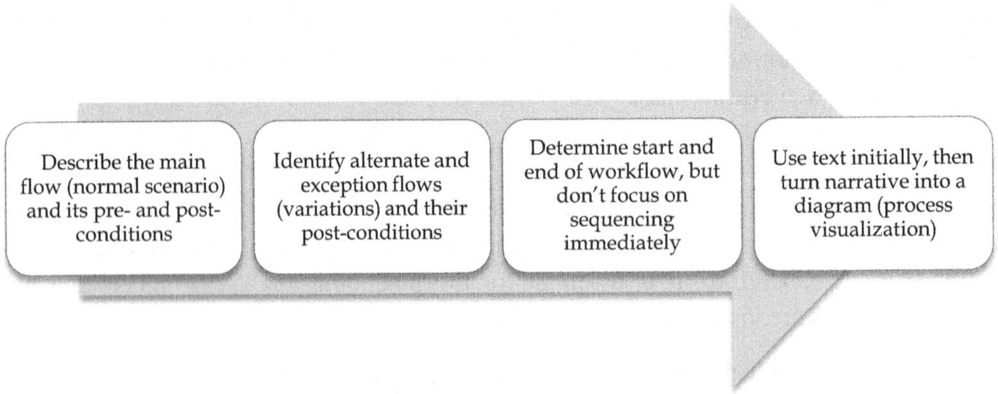

FIGURE 7-1. WORKFLOW AND PROCESS MODELING STEPS

Representing Activities

Each step in the process is described as an activity. If an activity cannot be further decomposed it is actually termed an action, although that distinction of generally of little practical consequence for business process modeling. Each activity is described with a verb-phrase, *e.g.*, "print loan request form".

Table 7-1 below summarizes the different activity symbols for both UML and BPMN.

An automated activity is indicated with the stereotype *«automated»*. It means that the activity is carried out using a system, that it requires a system, or that it is done completely by a system. On the other hand, a manual activity is indicated with the stereotype *«manual»*. It indicates an activity that is done manually by a person without the use of a system.

An activity representing a task to be carried out by one workflow participant is graphically shown as a rounded corner rectangle.

Sequencing of activities is indicated with control flows (edges). You should only have one input and output flow per activity; use merges and joins when combining multiple control flows.

Activities in the workflow sequence are connected by a solid line with an open arrow in UML and a solid line with a closed arrow in BPMN. The activities themselves therefore do not need to be numbered.

TABLE 7-1. UML AND BPMN ACTIVITY AND CONTROL SYMBOLS

Element	UML	BPMN
Simple Activity	Activity	Activity
Automated Activity	«automated» AutomatedActivity	«automated» AutomatedActivity
Manual Activity	«manual» ManualActivity	«manual» ManualActivity
Control Flow	ActivityA → ActivityB	ActivityA → ActivityB

Indicating Process Start and End

The start (source) of a process and the ends (sinks) of a process must be clearly indicated. There can only be one start for each process, but there may be multiple ends as there are successful as well as possibly multiple failed terminations. The control flow points from the initial activity icon (*i.e.*, start or source) to the first activity.

The process end symbols can be optionally labeled. One use of the label is to indicate whether the process ended successfully or whether it failed to meet the post conditions.

TABLE 7-2. PROCESS TERMINALS IN UML AND BPMN

Element	UML	BPMN
Start (Source)		
End (Sink)		

Showing Pre- and Post-Conditions

Pre-conditions summarize the assumptions that the process designer makes. Furthermore, pre-conditions indicate constraints that must be true in order for the process to be completed successfully.

Stereotypes are a general UML and BPMN mechanism for classifying constructs. All stereotypes are shown between « and ». We have already seen the «*automated*» and «*manual*» stereotypes for activities. Here we use stereotypes to classify notes as either pre-conditions or post-conditions.

Constraints, such as pre- and post-conditions, are placed between curly braces, *e.g.*, *{pre-condition}*.

Post-conditions summarize the outcome of the process. They are primarily concerned about changes to data or output and they are critical for testing.

TABLE 7-3. PRE- AND POST-CONDITIONS

Element	UML	BPMN
Pre-Condition		
Post-Condition		

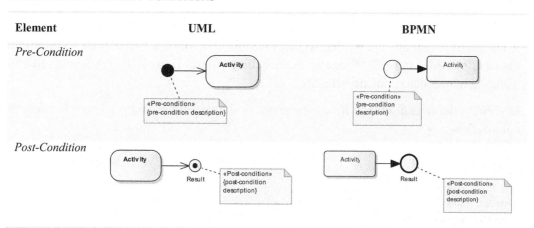

Illustrating Workflow Divergence

Many times during a workflow, some condition may occur that causes the flow to branch and different activities are carried out in response. In UML and BPMN, a decision (called a gateway in BPMN) is shown graphically with a diamond shaped icon from which at least two control flows emanate. Each control flow is tagged with the condition that would cause the flow to proceed in that direction. This is different from the classic flow chart approach where the decision icon contains a question that is either affirmed or negated ("yes" or "no" labels on the branches are the most common way to show this in a flow chart.) The approach in UML and BPMN makes it possible to have more than two outgoing control flows from a decision.

The labels on the outgoing control flows are called *guard conditions* in the notation vernacular and are placed into a pair of square brackets ('[…]') in UML but not BPMN. The naming of the guard condition can be formal or informal – there is no prescriptive format for the writing of the guard conditions. For business analysis, it is best to keep the guard conditions simple and expressed in a narrative form.

The guard conditions on the decision must be mutually exclusive and at least one condition along one of the control flows must be true otherwise the process halts. Each control must be labeled with a guard condition. Exclusivity means that only one of the activities after the branch will execute. This is the reason why the basic branch is called an exclusive gateway in BPMN.

The path that should be taken if none of the conditions match can be indicated using the simple condition [*else*] or [*otherwise*].

If the guard conditions are written so that multiple conditions are true, then according to the rules of UML and BPMN one of the matching control flows will be taken at random resulting in non-deterministic behavior.

In BPMN, the default branch for a divergence is shown with a slash (/) across the default control flow.

Element	UML	BPMN
Exclusive divergence or branch; also known as an exclusive gateway in BPMN	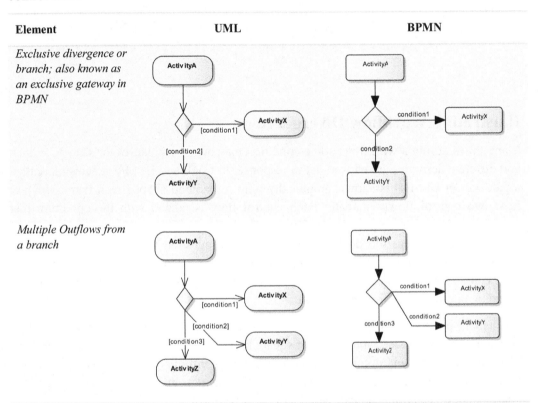	
Multiple Outflows from a branch		

Subflows must be merged explicitly when they converge back into a single flow. UML and BPMN use the same symbols for branch and merge, which might be confusing at first to some readers. It is easy to distinguish; however, as branches have multiple outgoing flows while merges have multiple incoming flows. See Table 7-4 for an illustration of the notation.

UML 2 requires merges, while UML 1 did not. Optionally, color can be used to help distinguish the two, although color has no defined semantics in either BPMN or UML.

TABLE 7-4. MERGING CONVERGENT FLOWS

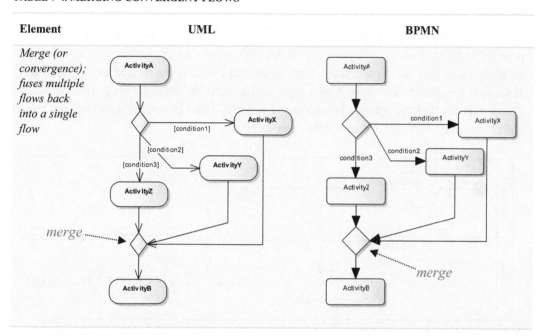

In some situations, when for example the merge symbol is confusing stakeholders even after thorough explanation, it is acceptable to eliminate the merge and directly connect the control flows to *ActivityB*.

Assigning Activities to Participants

Partitions (or pools in BPMN) are used to indicate who performs which activity in a process. Partitions can be horizontal, vertical, or both. Partitions are labeled with the process participant who is responsible for carrying out the activities (tasks) in that partition. If a participant has to make a decision, the branch icon must be shown in that participant's partition.

Partitions and pools are generally arranged horizontally, although in UML partitions can also be drawn vertically. Partitions can be subdivided into lanes to illustrate who within a group performs an activity. Figure 7-2 shows partitioning in UML, while Figure 7-3 illustrates pooling in BPMN.

Group Activities

An activity can only be placed into one partition or pool and therefore an activity can only be assigned to one participant. If an activity is done by more than one person, then an abstract participant representing a group or team should be created and the partition should be the group. To show which parts of the activity are done by a member of the group requires that the activity be explained in more detail in a separate workflow model which contains partitions for each team member.

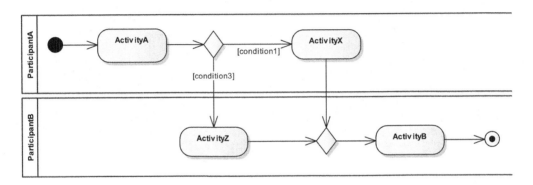

FIGURE 7-2. PROCESS PARTITIONING IN UML

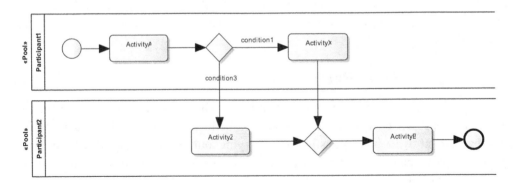

FIGURE 7-3. PROCESS PARTITIONING IN BPMN WITH POOLS

UML also supports traditional vertical swimlanes in addition to horizontal partitions. The main benefit of partitions is that they can be subdivided into lanes, while swimlanes cannot. However, some stakeholders may feel more comfortable with swimlanes.

Managing Complexity

Document the process at a very high level first, keeping it to 7-10 structured activities. Refine each structured activity into a separate sub-process. Continue layering until you have only actions, *i.e.*, activities which can be carried out by a single actor in a short amount of time.

UML uses composite activities to hide complexity and to group related activities within a process, while BPMN uses process nodes.

The UML example in Figure 7-4 below shows a workflow with several activities. The activity *ComplexActivity* is a composite activity (note the composition symbol in the lower right corner of the icon.) The details of how *ComplexActivity* works is shown in a separate, but linked, workflow diagram. Modeling tools automatically link the main workflow to the lower level workflows.

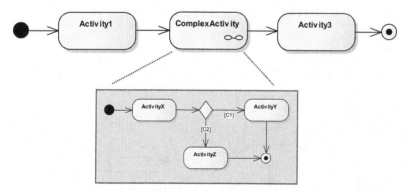

FIGURE 7-4. HIERARCHICAL DECOMPOSITION WITH UML COMPOSITE ACTIVITIES

This hierarchical decomposition approach manages complexity at each level. After all, not everyone needs to know how everything works.

The BPMN mechanism for hierarchically layering complex workflows is identical to UML.

Grouping Related Activities

In large processes it becomes useful to show which activities form a logical group of related activities. In UML the structured activity is used, while in BPMN we apply a group.

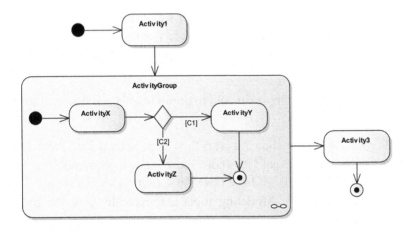

FIGURE 7-5. GROUPING RELATED ACTIVITIES IN UML

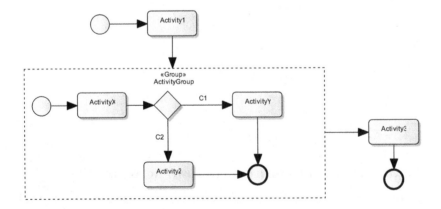

FIGURE 7-6. GROUPING RELATED ACTIVITIES IN BPMN

Unordered and Parallel Steps

In certain situations, a set of activities needs to be performed, but the actual order in which the activities are performed does not matter. This is modeled in UML with a *fork/join* pair, while in BPMN we use a *parallel inclusive gateway*. The notational elements are summarized in Table 7-5 below. In UML, the first synchronization bar is called the *fork*, while the second one that merges the path back together is called a *join*. Note that in BPMN, the same icon is used for the join as was used to split the workflow.

The actual semantics is defined such that the activities can be done in any order or at the same time (in parallel.) However, all of the activities between the split and the join must occur before the process proceeds.

The outgoing control flows can be conditional in which case only those flows that meet the guard condition are performed. In this case the semantics of the join is such that it will only wait for all started activities. If none of the conditions are met, then none of the activities will be performed and the workflow proceeds with activity immediately after the join.

TABLE 7-5. INCLUSIVE, CONDITIONAL, AND COMPLEX SPLITS IN UML AND BPMN

Element	UML	BPMN
Inclusive Split (all paths are taken in any order)	*fork and join*	*parallel inclusive gateway*

Element	UML	BPMN

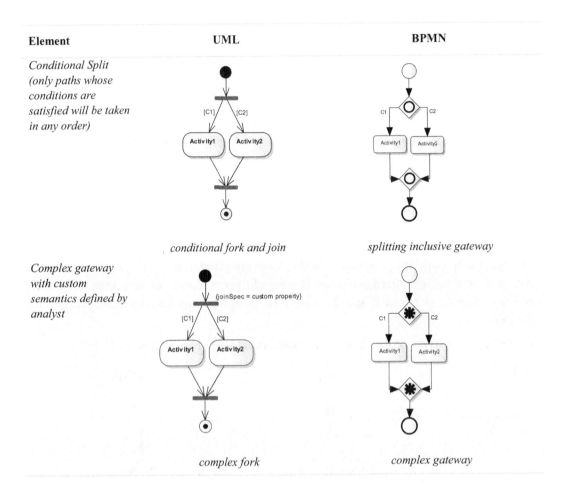

Conditional Split (only paths whose conditions are satisfied will be taken in any order)

conditional fork and join

splitting inclusive gateway

Complex gateway with custom semantics defined by analyst

complex fork

complex gateway

Iteration and Repeating Steps

Iterations, *i.e.*, activities that are repeated, are generally indicated with expansion regions in UML: dotted boxes placed around the repeating activities. In BPMN they are indicated with looping activities.

In UML, the "loop condition" is generally indicated with a note. If the iteration is over some set of objects or data values, then a three-part box is added to the expansion region and the box is labeled with the data set over which the iteration occurs. The steps within the region are applied to each element of the data set.

Note that the activities within the expansion region form a self-contained sub-workflow with their own source and sink, although the final symbol is a flow final rather than a process final.

A stereotype in the expansion region is used to indicate the iteration semantics:

«**iterative**»: one iteration at a time

«**concurrent**»: all iterations are happening at the same time

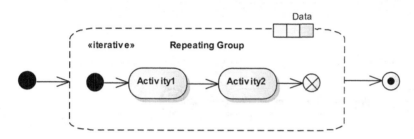

FIGURE 7-7. REPEATED STEPS IN UML WITH EXPANSION REGION

Object Flows

Data flows are called object flows in UML and BPMN. Object flows bring the value of data flow diagramming to UML and BPMN. Object flows show tangible or intangible objects that are generated and consumed by activities. This provides activity diagrams with capabilities similar to DFDs.

Objects are graphically illustrated with square-corner boxes in UML and dog-earned boxes similar to notes in BPMN. The name of the generated or used object is written inside the box and optionally underlined. Alternately, objects can be placed as "*nodes*" on the activities.

See Figure 7-8 and Figure 7-9 for examples of object flows in UML and BPMN. In that example, *Activity1* produces the object named *Object* which is then used again by *Activity3*.

Any object flowing into an activity must be generated somewhere. Any object generated by an activity must be used somewhere. The object does not have to be created or used within the same diagram, only within the same model.

The details of the objects are shown in a *UML Class Diagram*. Every object shown on an activity diagram must be an instance of a class contained in some class diagram.

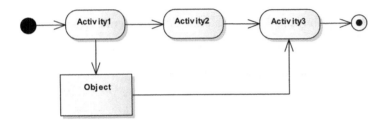

FIGURE 7-8. OBJECT FLOWS IN UML

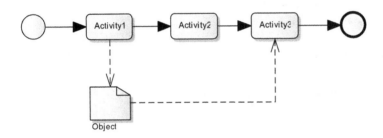

FIGURE 7-9. OBJECT FLOWS IN BPMN

Often, one activity produces data that is used by the immediately following activity, *i.e.*, the first activity produces the object that the second activity requires as input. There are two approaches in UML to indicate direct object consumption. Figure 7-10 illustrates the use of object nodes as the preferred style of direct object transfer.

FIGURE 7-10. OBJECT NODES IN UML

A third approach for specifying data flows between activities is to place the name of the objects on the control flow. Be sure not to place them into square brackets as that would indicate a condition rather than a data flow. Although unorthodox, this labeling approach is acceptable in both UML and BPMN and is illustrated in Figure 7-11.

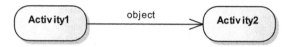

FIGURE 7-11. OBJECT FLOWS AS LABELS ON CONTROL FLOWS

Best Practices for Process Modeling

Be realistic: you can't capture everything and everything is not equally important

Be agile, but maintain an appropriate amount of rigor

Model collaboratively in teams (analysis is a social activity)

Use whiteboards to think; Use tools to record

Work iteratively

Stay focused on one business process at a time

Translate diagrams during validation meetings

Layer: don't try to put everything into a single workflow diagram

A model is an abstraction of reality that omits distracting detail

---

Indicating State Changes

The outcome of an activity may be a change in state (status) of an object, rather than the creation of a new object. The state of an object is indicated within square brackets underneath the name of the object in both UML and BPMN. In UML diagram in Figure 7-12 below, *Activity1* creates a new *Object* with state *StateA* which is immediately fed to *Activity2*. Within *Activity2*, the state of the *Object* is changed from *StateA* to *StateB*.

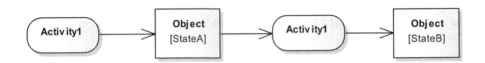

FIGURE 7-12. OBJECT STATE INDICATIONS IN UML

Complex state change rules of objects should be illustrated by *UML State Diagrams*. For more information on how document states with state diagrams, see Chapter 9. Note that BPMN does not support state diagrams.

Signals and Events

Signals indicate that another process should start and run while the current process continues. The name of the signal and the event must be the same to indicate that the signal causes the waiting processes to start. The symbols for events and signals are summarized in Table 7-6.

TABLE 7-6. SEND AND RECEIVED EVENTS AND SIGNALS IN UML AND BPMN

Element	UML	BPMN
Signal (Send)	EventA	▲
Event (Receive)	EventA	△
Timed Event	TimedEvent	🕐

The event becomes a process start that is timed and conditional. It starts only when the signal is sent. A process can also start based on a timed event, *i.e.*, when a certain amount of time has elapsed or some specific point in time has been reached.

A signal can start multiple processes if they are all waiting for the same event.

The UML example in Figure 7-13 illustrates the following process. Activity1 is the first step in the workflow carried out by Participant1. After *Activity1* has completed signal

"*EventA*" is sent to any waiting process. As soon as the signal has been sent, *Activity2* is executed. In the meantime, *Participant2* starts to carry out *ActivityX* followed by *ActivityY* without waiting for *Participant1*. The two processes are running simultaneously. If you need *Participant1* to know when *Participant2* is done, then you could have *Participant2* issue another signal that *Participant1* waits for.

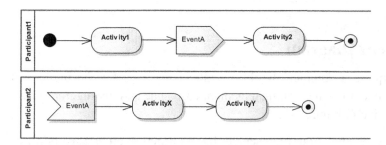

FIGURE 7-13. SIGNALS AND EVENTS IN UML

BPMN has a much richer messaging than UML and in this chapter we only considered those aspects of BPMN that are also available in UML.

Text Notes

It is unlikely that every insight can be captured conveniently in either UML or BPMN. While both notations are rich in their expressive power, it is sometimes easier and simpler if certain process insights are documented as notes. The UML and BPMN text annotation icons are shown in Table 7-7 below.

Notes are linked to the modeling element they annotate through a dashed line.

TABLE 7-7. UML AND BPMN TEXT ANNOTATIONS

Element	UML	BPMN
Text Note	Text Annotation	Text Annotation

Linking a Note to an Element

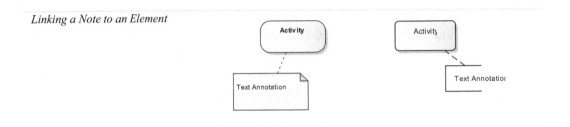

Annotated Workflow Diagram

The diagrams below express a complete workflow model in UML for the process of providing funding to a student for the loan management case. The activity diagrams are a visualization of the narrative in Figure 5-1.

The workflow model is layered and represented by multiple – progressively more detailed – workflow diagrams. First, a high-level summary of the workflow is presented. Then, each step in the high-level workflow is refined into separate workflow diagrams. Note that the loan administrator and officer are initially combined into the abstract participant "financial aid organization." The participant model in Figure 7-14 describes the relationships between the participants. It is essentially an organization model, but not from the perspective of a reporting structure, but rather a collaboration structure.

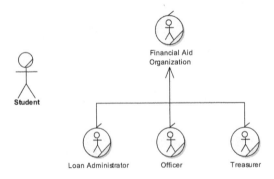

FIGURE 7-14. EXAMPLE OF PARTICIPANT MODEL

Notice how the diagrams are labeled with a numeric identifier (consistent with the other process model, of course), title, perspective ("as-is" vs. "to-be"), and level (summary or detailed).

It is not unusual that during the construction of the workflow diagram additional insights as well as previous oversights are uncovered. This demonstrates the complementary nature of diagrams and narratives.

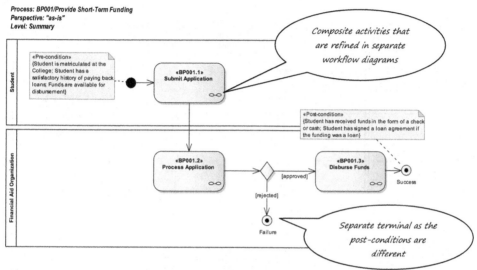

FIGURE 7-15. EXAMPLE OF SUMMARY WORKFLOW MODEL (BP001)

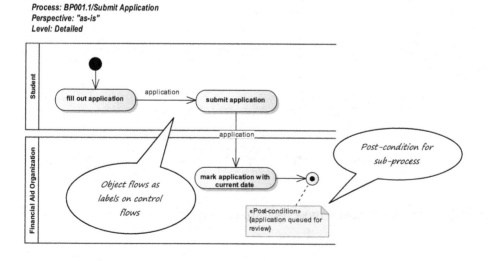

FIGURE 7-16. EXAMPLE OF DETAILED WORKFLOW MODEL (BP001.1)

Process: BP001.2/Process Application
Perspective: "as-is"
Level: Detailed

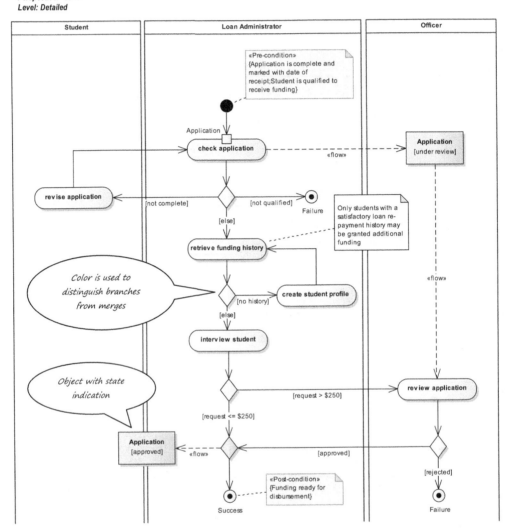

FIGURE 7-17. EXAMPLE OF DETAILED WORKFLOW MODEL (BP001.2)

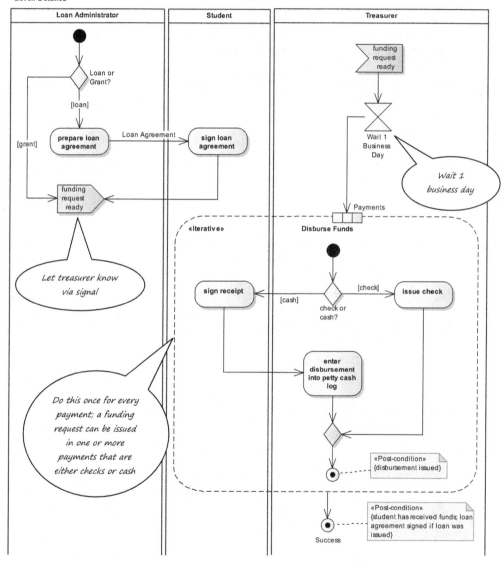

Process: BP001.3/Disburse Funds
Perspective: "as-is"
Level: Detailed

FIGURE 7-18. EXAMPLE OF DETAILED WORKFLOW MODEL (BP001.3)

Summary

- UML and BPMN offer a rich notation for documenting complex workflows
- Both notations have the capability to indicate activity sequencing, parallel and conditional activities, concurrent workflows, sub-workflows, activity grouping, object flows, and timed events

8 BUSINESS RULES

Chapter Objectives

- Define business rules
- Construct a business rule catalog
- Document business rules using structured narratives and tables

During elicitation a business analyst will not only discover process activities but also business rules (or rules for short). According to the Business Rules Group, a business rule describes a policy, guideline, standard, or regulation by which the business operates[8]. It is a statement that defines or constrains some aspect of the business and is intended to assert business structure, or to control or influence the behavior of business processes.

Rules should be atomic, *i.e.*, they should not be further decomposable, and they may not be process-dependent. They are commonly documented using structured narratives and tables.

Some examples of rules for the loan management system case:

- *Only matriculated students may obtain funding.*
- *Only students with a satisfactory loan re-payment history may be granted additional funding.*

---

[8] Business Rules Group (2000), *Defining Business Rules – What Are They Really?* Final Report, Revision 1.3, July 2000.

- *An officer must approve any funding request in excess of $250.*

Rules are not requirements, rather they assert constraints by which a company or organization conducts its business. By necessity, any process must comply with these rules. However, the business rules are independent of the process, although they are often enforced by the process.

There are a number of useful techniques for analyzing and documenting rules:

- Structured Narratives
- Decision Tables
- Decision Trees
- Domain Data Models
- Statecharts

This chapter looks at structured narratives and decision tables, while other chapters in this book explain data models and statecharts.

Finding Rules

Rules are generally discovered during process elicitation, but can also be identified when building workflow and other process model artifacts such as statecharts or domain data models.

Continually look out for references to rules and document the rules separately rather than burying them in the different process models. The rule catalog should become a separate artifact.

Documenting Business Rules

Rules must be thoroughly documented and should include its salient properties, such as definition, source, stability, applicability, and exceptions. Figure 8-1 shows a documentation template, although a matrix format can also be used. The rules are collected in a separate artifact called a rule catalog.

Title:	*A short description of the rule*
Identifier:	*Unique identifier, ideally starting with the prefix BR*
Definition:	*Full definition of the rule*

Example:	Short example of the rule or a situation in which it applies
Source:	The source of the rule; could be a stakeholder, domain expert, business document, or regulatory document
Related Rules:	Links to other rules that are similar to this one
Stability:	A statement whether the rule is likely to change in the near or long term
Applicability:	In which process or under which circumstances is this rule applicable
Exceptions:	Any exceptions to this rule

FIGURE 8-1. DOCUMENTATION TEMPLATE FOR RULES

Figure 8-2 describes an example of a rule for the loan management case.

Title:	**A loan may be paid out in multiple disbursements**
Identifier:	BR012 (Disbursing Loans)
Definition:	A student may receive several installments of a loan. Each installment or disbursement is added to the loan principal.
Example:	Mary Anderson receives tuition assistance for all four years at State College. The four "loans" she receives all, in fact, disbursements of a single loan.
Source:	Financial Aid
Related Rules:	BR007: Disbursing Grants
Stability:	Not expected to change; change only possible with approval by College Board
Applicability:	Global
Exceptions:	If the student receives a loan during the last semester, then the loan must be issued as a single disbursement

FIGURE 8-2. EXAMPLE BUSINESS RULE DEFINITION

Rule Writing Guidelines

A well written rule is:

- cohesive and non-compound, *i.e.*, it describes a single rule which makes rules more reusable and easier to validate
- expressed in a form that is easy to understand by business stakeholders, domain experts, business analysts, and programmers

- augmented by decision tables, decision trees, and visual models
- intrinsic to the business and not specific to one system
- expressed independently from its enforcement
- declarative not procedural, *i.e.*, state the rule not how to enforce it

Types of Business Rules

There are a number of different types of business rules include the following:

- Definitions of business terms
- Business conditions and actions
- Data integrity constraints
- Mathematical and functional derivations
- Logical inferences
- Processing sequences
- Relationships among facts about the business

Structured Narratives

Structured narratives are a modified form of natural language for precisely specifying rules and procedures. It uses a subset of a natural language that is limited to: action verbs, noun phrases, but no adjectives or adverbs. It should read like a natural language such as English, but there are no specific standards:

Structured narratives use specific phrasing to document rules. For example:

> ***It must always hold that*** *the repayment date of a short-term loan is one month prior to the recipient's graduation date.*

Decision Tables

A decision table is a tabular representation of all conditions that affect some action. It contains an exhaustive list of conditions. The table can be arranged vertically or horizontally. A decision table provides for an accounting of all combinations of factors. It aids during elicitation and ensures that all scenarios are considered. They are ideal when multiple factors can occur simultaneously. Additionally, they are a foundation for writing test cases.

The decision table is a common documentation strategy used by analysts when documenting complex conditional rules:

- easier to visualize combinations of factors
- compact presentation of factors
- easier to spot mistakes and omissions
- groups related rules into a single representational structure
- translatable into a system executable form

Figure 8-3 below shows an example of a decision table summarizing rules regarding loan and grant eligibility for the loan management case. Here are the rules encoded in the table:

- *Students in their last semester cannot receive loans only grants*
- *Students must be matriculated to be eligible for any funding*
- *Students must be current on any loans that they have already received to be eligible for any other funding*

		1	2	3	4	5	6	7	8
Factors	Last Semester?	Y	Y	Y	Y	N	N	N	N
	Matriculated?	Y	Y	N	N	Y	Y	N	N
	Current on all Loans?	Y	N	Y	N	Y	N	Y	N
Actions	Eligible for Loan					x			
	Eligible for Grant	x				x			

FIGURE 8-3. DECISION TABLE

A decision table is a matrix representation of the complete set mutually exclusive conditional factors for some related set of rules.

Constructing a Decision Table

Start by defining the conditions or factors that determine the actions. Each condition must contain a subject, domain, and states. Next, define a list of possible actions. Formally, a decision table is a relation that maps conditions to actions.

For each condition determine number of possibilities (n) which can be binary (yes/no, true/false) or higher order. Then calculate the product of each condition's possibility cardinality to arrive at the total number of conditions. Write the conditions as columns in the decision table and number them from 1 to X.

So, if you have three factors in Figure 8-3 you would have three binary (yes/no) factors. Each has two possible outcomes and therefore there are $2*2*2 = 8$ possible combinations of conditions. Next, eliminate illegal combinations and then populate the table. Meet with the subject matter experts and complete the actions for each combination of factors. If you have too many conditions, write several tables to simplify each table.

Figure 8-4 lists the steps involved in constructing a decision table.

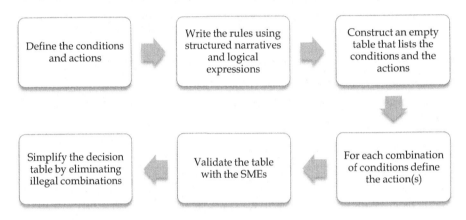

FIGURE 8-4. DECISION TABLE CONSTRUCTION STEPS

Technique Selection Guide

The table below summarizes the different techniques for documenting business rules and when to use them.

TABLE 8. BUSINESS RULE DOCUMENTATION TECHNIQUE SELECTION GUIDE

Technique	Applicability
Structured Narratives	clarity and readability are paramount and stakeholders must be able to easily validate the rules
Decision Tables	complex combinations of factors, actions, and rules are present and you need to effectively show all legal combinations
Decision Trees	sequence of conditions and actions is critical or when not every condition is appropriate or you need a visual representation of a decision table

Technique	Applicability
State Charts	single term (entity) is subject to complex temporal rules
Data Models	complex relationships and constraints on multiple terms (entities) exist

Linking Rules to Processes and Activities

Rules must be linked to the activities that are governed by them. Construct a matrix that lists processes, activities, and their related rules.

TABLE 9. RULE/ACTIVITY TRACEABILITY MATRIX

Process	Activity	Applicable Rules
BP001.3	funding request ready	BR001; BR012
BP001.3	issue check	BR012

Summary

- Business rules (or rules for short) describe policies, guidelines, standards, or regulations by which the business operates
- Processes are subject to rules
- Rules must be documented separately from the processes
- Structured narratives and decision tables are two common approaches to documenting rules concisely

9   STATE MODELING

Chapter Objectives

- Visualize complex rules based on object states
- Construct statechart diagrams in UML
- Learn how to exploit statechart as a supporting model

State chart diagrams (or simply state diagrams or statecharts for short) are an important tool in business analysis. They are principally used to model the behavior of an entity/object but can also be used to show the state of a system or process activity.

A statechart is a visual description of a state machine. UML state diagrams are an implementation of *Harel Statecharts* which allow the modeling of concurrent and nested states as opposed to classic disjunctive state machines. BPMN does not support statecharts.

A statechart is a supporting model for a process. It is used only when objects are involved in the process and those objects have complex rules based on the state (or status) of the object.

Definition of a State

A state is a *stage in the lifetime* of an object (entity). A state is also often referred to as *status* or *code*.

States are represented by:

- a flag, or
- the values of a set of attributes

There are two special types of states in a statechart: the start state and the final state. The start state is the initial state an object is in when it is first created or comes into existence. The final state (also called a terminal or stop state) is the last state an object is in and it cannot change from that state to any other state.

A statechart may only have one start state but can have multiple final states.

State Transitions

A transition is a progression from one state to another triggered by some external or internal event. Transitions are named with verb phrases as they indicate an action or event.

Naming States

States should be named with an adjective as they are qualifiers. State names should be simple and reflect the business terminology. During elicitation listen for adjectives or status flags such as:

- an *approved* loan application
- a *disbursed* loan
- an *overdrawn* funding account

Watch for Questionable States

States that have transitions going into it, but none going out are final or terminal states. Similarly, states that have transitions emanating, but none going into it are start states.

Of course, states that have neither incoming nor outgoing transitions are not needed and should be eliminated from the statechart.

Be careful that states are not confused with activities; they have a very similar UML symbol. Any state that is named with a verb phrase and not an adjective is likely an activity rather than a state. Use a UML activity diagram to document the activity sequences not a statechart.

State Matrix

To find the transitions, construct a matrix listing all of the discovered states along the rows and the columns. Assume that the states along the rows are the source state and that the columns are the destination (or sink) state. Then ask: is it possible to get from state A to state B? If so, place an X in that cell. Then ask: what has to happen for that state change to occur? Replace the X with the event or action that causes the state change. Finally, visualize the state matrix with a statechart. Each cell becomes a transition.

Figure 9-1 illustrates the concept of a state matrix by showing the states and allowed transitions for an application in the loan management system case based on the business process "Provide Short-Term Funding." For example, an application that is "new" goes to the "under review" state once a loan administrator starts to review the application. According to the business rules, it would not be possible to directly disburse a funding request without first approving it. An application that is "under review" can go back to being "submitted" perhaps when the application was not filled out correctly.

	New	Submitted	Under Review	Approved	Rejected
New		X			
Submitted			X		
Under Review		X		X	X
Approved					
Rejected					

FIGURE 9-1. STATE MATRIX

In the above state matrix, the states "rejected" and "approved" appear to be terminal or final states as they don't transition to any other state. The state "new" does not have any incoming transitions, so it likely is the start state.

When to Create Statecharts?

Statecharts should be created for any "interesting" object:

- different rules apply depending on which state the object is in
- business tracks the status for an object
- object is being processed differently depending on its state

Statechart Elements

A *statechart* shows the *lifecycle* of an object:

- the states that an object can be in
- the events that cause state changes
- the actions that result from state changes

A single statechart represents a composite view of the dynamic aspects of a single object across all processes. In both UML and BPMN we document the state of an object that is used in a workflow by placing the state in brackets ([*state*]) underneath the object name. When you find yourself tracking the state in a workflow diagram, then you should create a statechart to fully explain the state model of the object.

UML State Symbol

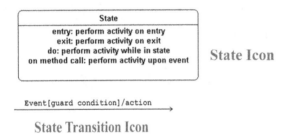

State Icon

State Transition Icon

Start and Stop States

A statechart can contain two special states:

- start state: beginning of the state machine (source)
- final state: stop or terminal state (sink)

There can only be one start state but there may be multiple end states and even possibly none.

Initial or Start State

Final or Stop State

Simple Statechart

The statechart in Figure 9-2 below is for an application from the loan management case. It is essentially a visualization of the state matrix of Figure 9-1. The simple statechart does not have any events on the transitions explaining why the transition occurs. While this is acceptable during early analysis, we need to eventually clarify under what conditions an object changes state. There is typically some processing that occurs that causes the object to change state.

The statechart in Figure 9-3 contains the events that cause transitions from one state to another. It explains the business rules more precisely.

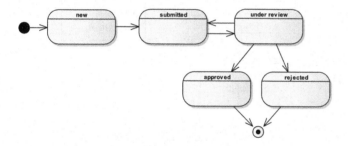

FIGURE 9-2. SIMPLE STATECHART

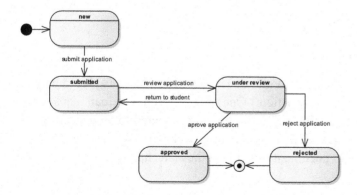

FIGURE 9-3. STATECHART WITH TRANSITION EVENTS

Reflexive Transitions

To show that some event is allowed only while an object is in a certain state even though the object does not change state when that event occurs is illustrated with a reflexive (or self) transition, *i.e.*, a transition from a state to itself. For instance, an application for funding that exceeds $250 must be reviewed by an officer. The application is still considered to be "under review" regardless of who is reviewing the application. However, only applications "under review" go to the officer. Figure 9-4 illustrates this concept.

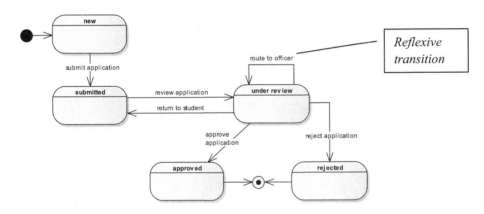

FIGURE 9-4. REFLEXIVE TRANSITIONS

Conditional Transitions

A condition on a transition is shown with a guard. The guard condition is placed between brackets after the event (and before any action.) One of the rules in our loan management case is that any application for more than $250 in funding is routed to an officer. So, the reflexive transition should be qualified to only occur when the request exceeds that amount. Figure 9-5 shows how to document this rule in the statechart.

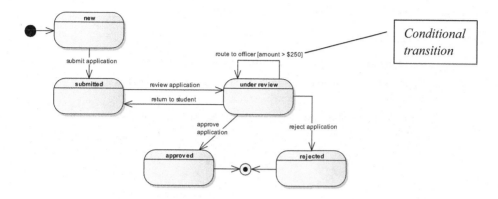

FIGURE 9-5. CONDITIONAL TRANSITIONS

Actions

UML allows actions to be attached to a state or to a transition to indicate that something happens either when you are going to, exiting from, or are in some state. Table 9-1 summarizes the different types of actions that can be placed on a state. Note that you can have multiple actions of each kind, for example two entry actions, three do actions, and four exit actions to indicate multiple activities that will occur in that state.

The example in Figure 9-6 documents several actions:

- when an application is under review, we check completeness of the application and student qualification
- once an application is approved we disburse the loan

Note that the action of disbursing a loan once the application is approved could have been done as either an entry action on the "approved" state or an action on the transition from "under review" to "approved".

The actions are directly derived from the processes in which the object participates and must be consistent with those processes. Create the statechart in conjunction with the workflow models and continually cross-check the models. The benefit is that oversights and misunderstandings are driven out through this process of checks-and-balances.

TABLE 9-1. ACTION TYPES ON STATES AND THEIR SEMANTICS

Action Type	Semantics
Entry	Perform this action upon any entry to the state
Exit	Perform this action upon exit from the state after some event has occurred
Do	Perform this action continually while in that state or until the action has completed

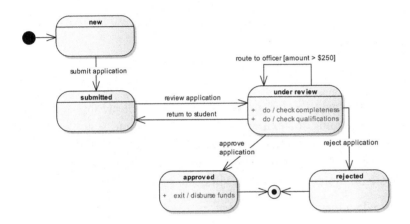

FIGURE 9-6. STATES WITH ACTIONS

Nested States

At the moment, the statecharts developed thus far do not distinguish between an application being under review by the loan administrator or the loan officer. In fact, the state "under review" has two substates: "assigned to loan administrator" and "assigned to officer". However, regardless who is reviewing the application it is "under review."

To show common characteristics of a group of states, we can place those states within another state as substates. The enclosing state is called the superstate. Figure 9-7 shows how to create a set of substates within a superstate.

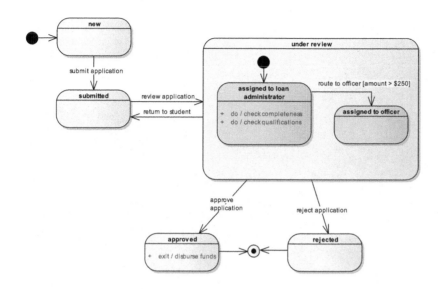

FIGURE 9-7. SUPERSTATE WITH NESTED SUBSTATES

Workflows vs. Statecharts

Workflows and statecharts look very much alike and are often confused. They have very similar symbols and both show a flow, but a workflow model describes <u>one process</u> involving multiple objects while a statechart describes <u>one object</u> involved in multiple processes. The two models have a quite different intent even though the notation is visually similar. Be careful not to confuse the two.

Summary

- Statecharts are an effective, although advanced, mechanism to document complex business rules
- Statecharts must be consistent with other process models
- Constructing statecharts adds checks-and-balances to the modeling process
- Workflows are written for processes while statecharts are written for objects

10   DOMAIN DATA MODELING

Chapter Objectives

- Identify domain entities and business objects
- Construct visual domain data models
- Use domain data models to validate business rules

A domain data model defines the important objects of a business domain. Domain data models are described using a visual notation supported by text narratives and other artifacts. A data model of a business domain captures structural rules, relational constraints, and data requirements.

Examples of domain data requirements and rules expressed in a narrative format:

- *A loan can only be given to a single student.*

- *A student is only provided a single loan, but the loan amount can be received in several disbursements.*

- *For each loan, the system must track the amount, interest rate, and payment schedule.*

Identifying Business Objects

To start identifying business objects (also called business entities or business terms) simply extract the nouns from the process narratives and other process modeling artifacts. In addition, during process elicitation, listen for stakeholders mentioning:

- tangible objects (*e.g.*, application form, loan agreement, check)
- conceptual entities (*e.g.*, funding decision, student profile)
- roles (*e.g.*, student)

- incidents (*e.g.*, disbursement)
- organizations (*e.g.*, financial aid organization)

Names for business objects must reflect the term that is used by the business. Furthermore, it must be a:

- noun in the singular (*Student*, *Disbursement*)
- name that is most descriptive (perhaps *Recipient* instead of *Student*)
- term accepted in the business domain

Visualizing Domain Data Models

A domain data model can be described in a narrative format in a table of business objects. Such a table includes all of the important objects (entities or terms) in the business domain along with their attributes.

Visualizing a domain data model is often preferable as it is easier to detect missing information and it provides a mechanism to show relationships between the objects. A UML class diagram is used to visualize the business objects. A business object is represented using one of two different styles of icons (see Figure 10-1). The rectangular icon is the traditional UML icon for a "class". It shows the business object's name and its attributes, *i.e.*, the information that the business tracks about it. The other icon is an enhanced icon used for modeling business entities with their names only.

Visualizing Business Objects

The business entity style icon is preferable for modeling business objects as it visually differentiates business domain objects from system data entities. Although, the drawback of the business entity style icon is that it cannot show any attributes. Attributes must then be tracked in a table of business objects. Such a table is also often referred to as a data dictionary.

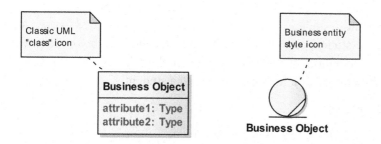

FIGURE 10-1. UML BUSINESS OBJECT SYMBOLS

Domain data modeling is an essential business analysis activity and the domain data model is part of the overall business architecture. The business analyst is expected to construct a domain data model illustrating the business objects while modeling processes. The domain data model defines the vocabulary of the business domain and reduces misunderstanding.

Visualizing Object Relationships

The business domain model is incrementally refined and initially details can be left vague. Eventually, the relationships and dependencies between business objects must be expressed. There are two main relationship types that are found among business objects:

- **Association**. A semantic link or dependency between objects, *e.g.*, a relationship between loan agreement and student to document the fact that a loan agreement is signed by a student.
- **Generalization**. A *type-of* relationship between objects, *e.g.*, a check is a type of disbursement.

Association Multiplicity

Every association relationship between two entities has an associated *multiplicity*. For example:

- *Every loan is disbursed in one or more disbursements.*
- *Every grant is given to a single student.*

Associations are visually represented as a solid line between two business objects. Multiplicity is shown through a numeric annotation in the form $n..m$, where n is the lower bound and *m* is the upper bound. Figure 10-2 illustrates this concept by visualizing the association between a loan and a student. It states that every loan is extended to one (and only one) student, although a student can receive multiple loans and possibly none (lower bound of 0.) Note that the association also has an optional label ("is extended to") with an indicator for the reading direction, *i.e.*, a loan is extended to a student.

The association is read as follows:

- Every loan is extended to one and only one student
- A student has extended to them zero or more loans

The '*' as the upper bound indicates that there is no specific upper limit on how many loans a student may receive. If the business rule is that a student cannot receive more than 10 loans, then the multiplicity would be written as '0..10'.

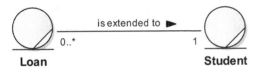

FIGURE 10-2. UML ASSOCIATION RELATIONSHIP WITH MULTIPLICITY

The example demonstrates that multiplicities are nothing more than graphical representations of domain business rules.

UML provides many more data modeling constructs, but these are beyond the scope of this book and fall outside the realm of business process modeling. Some of these constructs are aggregation, composition, role labels, foreign keys, unique identifiers, and constraints.

Generalization

Generalization defines a *type*-of or is-*a* relationship between business objects. For example, a check is a type of disbursement or loan administrator and treasurer are types of employees. In UML, generalization is visually indicated using a closed but unfilled arrow pointing from the specific type of the general type. Figure 10-3 illustrates the concept of generalization between business objects.

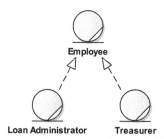

FIGURE 10-3. UML GENERALIZATION RELATIONSHIP

Validating Models

The process models developed when mapping a business process must be validated with the business experts and stakeholders. This includes all models: domain data models, workflow models, process narratives, and so forth. Validation is most commonly accomplished through walkthroughs and informal reviews. Reviews should be conducted as collaborative sessions.

Summary

- Domain data models define the business objects used in a process
- A complete data model includes objects, relationships, and multiplicities
- Multiplicities are visual representations of structural business rules

11 PERFORMANCE ANALYSIS

Chapter Objectives

- Calculate the execution time and cost of a process
- Remove bottlenecks
- Learn about process simulation

The final step in process modeling is the analysis of the performance of the process with the goal of identifying performance bottlenecks and ways to improve the time it takes to perform the process and reduce the cost of the process.

Process analysis is generally the responsibility of operation management specialists, although simple analysis is frequently done by business analysts as well.

There are two main goals in process performance analysis: determine how long a process takes to execute and how much it will cost. This chapter takes a look at some quantitative techniques for determining execution time and cost with the ultimate intent of identifying bottlenecks and choosing the optimal process design from a set of process alternatives.

When processes are being redesigned there are often multiple process redesign alternatives. It is the business analyst's responsibility to evaluate the different process redesigns and determine which one is optimal for some given business objective.

Calculating Time and Cost

To calculate the execution time and cost of a process, do the following:

- For each activity, determine execution time and cost
- If the activity is a composite activity, determine execution time and cost for each of the sub-activities and sum them

- Roll-up all execution time and cost estimates to arrive at a final estimate for each process

In this approach we assume that a process runs to completion and that while the process runs it is not started again. In other words, different process execution instances are not running concurrently. This is a significant simplification, but concurrent execution would require that we also analyze the queuing properties of each activity.

For example, let's say that during the process "Provide Short-Term Funding", the loan administrator checks an application for completeness. Is it realistic to assume that during that time another student cannot submit an application for funding? That is exactly what the requirement of a single execution instance states. Now if we allow multiple execution instances, then we would have to determine the execution time of an activity that takes into account that the person performing the activity is busy and that we have to wait – or queue the request. This implies that we need to know the average queue length, service time, and arrival rate of activity execution requests to determine the likely time it takes for an activity to be carried out. Such problems can be modeled using various queuing models and probability distributions for arrivals (Poisson being one of the most commonly used theoretical distributions). These types of analyses are generally approached with either Discrete Event or Monte Carlo simulation. Such performance analysis problems fall into the realm of operations management and are beyond the scope of this book. Furthermore, they require the use of special-purpose process simulation tools.

Process Parameters

To effectively calculate execution time and cost of a process, we need to collect the following metrics for each process element using the suggested sources:

Process Element	Metrics of Interest	Source of Metrics
Participant	• Cost per unit of time	Human Resources; Management; Contracts
Materials	• Cost per unit	Bills of Laden; Invoices; Price Catalog
Activity	• Length in units of time to carry out activity • Participant assigned to carry out the activity	Direct measurement through observation; Interviews

	• Materials needed to carry out the activity	
Decision	• Length in units of time required to make decision • Probabilities of each path	Direct measurement through observation; Interviews
Flow	• Length in units of time to transition from one activity to the next, including transport	Direct measurement through observation; Interviews

Estimates

For each process we need to calculate three estimates each for execution time and cost:

- **Worst case**: the most time it will take to run and the highest cost
- **Best case**: the least time it will take to run and the lowest cost
- **Expected case**: the expected time it will take on average and the average cost

These calculations can be done using a spreadsheet such as *Microsoft Excel* or a special-purpose process analysis tool such as *Savvion* or *ProVision*. The main difficulty in using a spreadsheet for analysis rather than a special-purpose tool is that as the process is revised and refined, the separate model must be kept up to date manually.

Figure 11-1 represents an Excel model for the process "Provide Short-Term Funding" from the loan management case. Note the use of nested activities to automate the roll-up and estimate calculation.

Also, the analysis is only concerned with the worst case. The calculations are based on the resource costs in Figure 11-2. The resources include the participants who carry out the activities and the materials that are used by some of the activities. The spreadsheet model in Figure 11-1 is based on these resource costs.

Task	Actor	Materials	Time (hr)		Cost (US$)		Total
			Longest	Time	Materials		
Submit Application			1.0167	$ 0.29	$ 0.08	$	0.37
fill out application	Student	Application Form	1.0000	$ -	$ 0.08	$	0.08
submit application	Student	None	0.0000	$ -	$ -	$	-
mark application	Loan Administrator	None	0.0167	$ 0.29	$ -	$	0.29
Process Application			6.5000	$ 75.00	$ -	$	75.00
check application	Loan Administrator	None	0.7500	$ 13.24	$ -	$	13.24
revise application	Student	None	1.0000	$ -	$ -	$	-
check completeness	Loan Administrator	None	0.5000	$ 8.82	$ -	$	8.82
check qualifications	Loan Administrator	None	0.5000	$ 8.82	$ -	$	8.82
retrieve funding history	Loan Administrator	None	0.5000	$ 8.82	$ -	$	8.82
create student profile	Loan Administrator	None	0.7500	$ 13.24	$ -	$	13.24
interview student	Loan Administrator	None	1.0000	$ 17.65	$ -	$	17.65
route application	Loan Administrator	None	0.2500	$ 4.41	$ -	$	4.41
review application	Officer	None	1.0000	$ -	$ -	$	-
make funding decision	Officer	None	0.2500	$ -	$ -	$	-
Disburse Funds (single disbursement)			3.4500	34.8529	0.0000	$	34.85
determine if loan or grant	Loan Administrator	None	0.0500	$ 0.88	$ -	$	0.88
prepare loan agreement	Loan Administrator	None	1.0000	$ 17.65	$ -	$	17.65
sign loan agreement	Student	None	0.1000	$ -	$ -	$	-
route funding request	Loan Administrator	None	0.1000	$ 1.76	$ -	$	1.76
wait until next business day	None	None	1.0000	$ -	$ -	$	-
sign receipt	Student	None	0.1000	$ -	$ -	$	-
issue check	Treasurer	None	0.5000	$ 6.62	*Cost of workers*		6.62
enter disbursements	Treasurer	None	0.5000	$ 6.62	$ -		6.62
hand check to student	Treasurer	None	0.1000	$ 1.32	$ -	$	1.32
Totals			**10.9667**	**$ 110.15**	**$ 0.08**	**$**	**110.23**

Longest time process will take

Total cost of process: worker time and materials

FIGURE 11-1. PROCESS PERFORMANCE ANALYSIS

	Unit	Cost Per Unit
Participants:		
Loan Administrator	Hour	$ 17.65
None	Hour	$ -
Officer	Hour	$ -
Student	Hour	$ -
Treasurer	Hour	$ 13.24
Materials:		
Application Form	Single	$ 0.08
Check	Single	$ 0.25

FIGURE 11-2. RESOURCE COSTS FOR PERFORMANCE ANALYSIS

Performance Optimization

Processes must be continually monitored and improved. When analyzing the performance of a process, consider the following questions for each activity within the process:

- Can the activity be eliminated and what would the consequence be?
- Can the activity be done in a simpler manner?
- Can the activity be combined with another activity and thus reduce transport cost or the time delay to route the work to another worker?
- Can the activity be split up into multiple activities that can be done in parallel or by less expensive resources
- Can the activity be re-assigned to a less expensive worker?
- Can the activity be automated through a machine or information system?

Task Splitting

Identify tasks that can be split into two or more activities some of which can be assigned to different participants who are less expensive per unit of time. This results in a reduction in the cost of the process, but may increase the overall process execution time because of the overhead in communicating between the parties and the time it may take to hand off work and transfer information or materials.

Resource Reassignment

Determine whether each activity is carried out by the least expensive and most efficient participant or if the activity could be handed off to someone else that is less expensive per unit of time or more efficient. Resource reassignment can result in a reduction in the cost of the process without necessarily increasing the overall process execution time.

Automation

For each activity in a workflow determine if the activity could be fully or at least partially done using a system and therefore decrease the cost of manual labor resulting in reduced process cost.

Summary

- Processes must be analyzed in terms of execution time and cost to determine which process re-design variant is best
- Execution time and cost are calculate for the worst, best, and expected case
- Resource splitting, resource reassignment, and automation are common approaches to improving process execution time and reduce process cost

REFERENCES & BIBLIOGRAPHY

For more information or to learn more about the topics addressed in this book, consult the following resources and visit our web site at www.cathris.com:

Business Rules Group (2000), Defining Business Rules – What Are They Really? Final Report, Revision 1.3, July 2000.

> *A seminal reference report on business rules.*

Fowler, M. (2004). UML Distilled, 3rd Edition. Addison-Wesley Pearson.

> *A great reference book on UML that's just detailed enough and not too confusing. Contains an explanation of all UML diagrams and is more geared towards developers.*

International Institute of Business Analysis Body of Knowledge (BABOK) v2.0, www.theiiba.com, 2009.

> *An encyclopedic collection of best practices for business analysis.*

Kratochvil, M., & McGibbon, B. (2003). UML xtra-light: How to Specify Your Software Requirements. Cambridge University Press.

> *A short book on UML that keeps to the essentials. Explains how to get from use cases to requirements and how to model the requirements with use case, activity, class, and state diagrams.*

Owen, J. (2004) Business Rules Management Systems, InfoWorld, June 2004.

> *A good introduction on how to document business rules and build systems around rules engines.*

Rinzler, B. (2009). Telling Stories: A Short Path to Writing Better Software Requirements. Wiley Publishing.

Short and concise book that provides a practical approach to writing good requirements documents that contains proper narratives and supporting diagrams.

Ross, R. (2003). Principles of the Business Rule Approach, Addison-Wesley Publishing.

An excellent treatment of business rules, how to encode them, and how to integrate information systems with business rules management systems.

Visual Modeling Forum, www.visualmodeling.com

Web forum for all visual modeling languages. Lists tools, notations, books, and other resources.

Wiegers, K. (2003). Software Requirements, 2nd Edition. Microsoft Press.

An excellent source of common sense approaches to eliciting, tracking, refining, and implementing software requirements.

INDEX

CPSIA information can be obtained
at www.ICGtesting.com
Printed in the USA
LVOW03s2239260116

472370LV00009B/215/P